Milestones of American Painting in our century

Milestones of
American Painting
in our century

FREDERICK S. WIGHT

Introduction by Lloyd Goodrich

with fifty illustrations
including twelve
in color

The Institute of Contemporary Art, Boston
CHANTICLEER PRESS NEW YORK

Published by

CHANTICLEER PRESS INCORPORATED

41 EAST 50TH STREET NEW YORK 22 NEW YORK

in association with

MAX PARRISH & CO LIMITED

ADPRINT HOUSE RATHBONE PLACE LONDON WI

1949

Designed and Produced by

ADPRINT LTD LONDON

Contents

Author's acknowledgment

The Institute and its collaborators extend their thanks to the many individuals and institutions who have generously made their paintings available for reproduction.

For their helpful assistance in the preparation of the present volume, the writer wishes to acknowledge a debt to Mr. Lloyd Goodrich and Mr. Bartlett H. Hayes, Jr.; to Mr. James S. Plaut, for editing the text; and to those writers whose books are mentioned in the bibliography. He is grateful for permission to quote the words of a number of painters which are drawn from the text of *Americans 1942* and *Fourteen Americans*, published by the Museum of Modern Art and edited by Miss Dorothy C. Miller; and he extends particular thanks to Miss Jane Bagg of the Institute staff for her loyal collaboration.

Errata

page 29. Painting no. 2 should read as follows: JOHN SLOAN / *McSorley's Back Room,* 1912. Oil, 26 × 32 / Present Owner: Dartmouth College, Hanover, New Hampshire.

page 36. For *McSorley's Bar* read *McSorley's Back Room.*

page 94, line 20. For *The Musicians* read *Music Maker.*

page 100, line 20. For "sixteenth-" read "eighteenth-century".

Introduction

As the twentieth-century nears its halfway mark we begin to see it in perspective. When it opened, American art was dominated by a lifeless academicism. European developments after impressionism were unknown here. But within a few years all this was changed. The Eight, though far from advanced in style, broke the academy's hold. Young Americans abroad discovered the ferment of modernism and brought it back with them. By the early 1920's modernism had won at least half its battle. But it was never to be as organized a movement as in Europe. For American artists the movement was a liberation and a starting-point for highly personal developments. Instead of the European experimentation with form, our leading tendency was towards emotional expressionism.

The victory of modernism produced its own reaction. Rejecting its abstract and internationalist tendencies, certain painters turned to picturing American life, renewing the viewpoint of the Eight but with more drastic realism and deeper insight. Then came the depression, turning younger artists towards social comment and satire.

In the past ten years the pendulum has again swung back towards the subjective and abstract. Surrealism has introduced a new psychological dimension into content. And there has been a revival of abstractionism, this time on a wider scale and with a broader philosophy which takes account of the values of subject-matter.

The past half-century of American art, in variety of viewpoints and styles, in richness of creative gifts, in freedom of expression forbidden to artists in authoritarian countries, has been the most vital period in our history. From the provincial backwaters of 1900 we have entered the main stream of world art.

This book, the product of an exhibition organized by Frederick S. Wight of the Institute of Contemporary Art, Boston, presents works by fifty outstanding painters of the period. The broad, representative selection, with Mr. Wight's illuminating survey and commentary, should go far towards enlarging our understanding of the times through which we have lived.

LLOYD GOODRICH
Associate Director,
Whitney Museum of American Art

Milestones of
American Painting in our century

The American Reporters

In nineteenth-century America, the appreciation of art came in through the library door; a hundred years ago the owners of libraries embellished them with copies of European painting and sculpture, undisturbed that these possessions were not originals: a copy of Raphael was as satisfactory as a copy of Shakespeare. Painting was subordinated to literature, and both arts were cast in a romantic mold. The end of the romantic period in Europe was approaching; but in America it was to persist. On the one hand the Americans lived out a social and political legend; on the other they were fascinated by their physical circumstances. These conditions set the pattern of romantic realism in American art, and they are still at work today.

Painting paralleled literary forms. It could be a biography if it were a portrait, or a drama, or a short story. But journalism was the form of writing closest to the scale and pace of America after the Civil War. Journalism expressed the American urge for impact, stridency and freedom.

During the first ten years of this century there was a radical change in American painting, but it was primarily in subject-matter, a change not in attitude toward painting but in attitude toward life. It was a journalist's revolution coming out of Philadelphia. John Sloan, George Luks, William Glackens and Everett Shinn were young illustrators on the *Philadelphia Press*, under the direction of the art editor Edward Davis, father of the abstract painter Stuart Davis. This group breathed the atmosphere of the city desk; they were at war with the waning decorum of the last century. On Thursday evenings they met at the studio of Robert Henri, a young teacher at the Pennsylvania Academy of Fine Arts. Henri had studied abroad—he had been to Paris. He encouraged the illustrators to become painters, and his energetic influence gave them direction. The group pivoted on Henri's personality. In the next few years they all drifted over to the larger center of New York. There Henri taught at the Chase School, the others worked on the New York papers and magazines, and their associations still held them together.

These painters looked at the city of New York with a reporter's eye. Painting the waterfront, the slum, the saloon, the restless life of sidestreet and alley, they found a style to correspond to their interests. It was not a new style, for it had its roots in French Impressionism and in Manet, but it served the purpose admirably. It was incisive, bold and direct.

These painters made war on the academic and on the evasions of Victorianism, but their art was still related to a literary trend. The novels of Frank Norris and Theodore Dreiser's *Sister Carrie* had administered a similar shock. Painters and writers alike were moved by a deepening human sympathy, and were becoming socially and politically conscious. Some of Sloan's best work was done for the old *Masses*, of which he was art editor. The new painters won a notoriety as radicals from a public apathetic to painting itself.

The group was giving expression to something astir in society as a whole. Nineteenth-century idealism had grown brittle with pretense, and the new century was creating new types, new ideals. It was the day of a self-expressionism such as Ibsen had heralded. There was little evaluation of what was expressed, if only it brought release. The battle with suffocating conventions was there to be waged.

In America this salutary defiance had taken a special turn. Here there was a glorification of burliness, and the frontiersman was made to do double duty as the type of the common man. Theodore Roosevelt set the style and created a national hero in the Rough Rider. Elbert Hubbard wrote the *Message to Garcia*, which swept the country as the legend of the self-reliant man. In paint, Luks and Bellows put the professional athlete on canvas; the tough guy was here—and here to stay.

Strongholds of convention were on the defensive and the National Academy was keeping its powder as dry as its tradition. It had suffered a revolt in 1877 when the Society of American Artists split away from it. But by 1906 the Society's blood had cooled, and it came home docilely to live with its parent. The next year, since the radicals had nowhere else to show, there were drastic rejections. Sloan, Luks and Glackens were victims, and Henri withdrew his own entries from the Academy in protest.

William Macbeth, the art dealer, asked Henri to get together for exhibition the work of a number of painters of his choice. Henri chose the original Philadelphia group, adding the Impressionists Prendergast and Lawson and the Romanticist Arthur B. Davies. Those eight painters, including Henri himself, were shown in 1908 in New York, Philadelphia and Chicago. The Eight had great plans for survival as an organized movement, but they never exhibited together again.

They were a motley and ill-assorted group; the proletarian art of Luks and Sloan and the refined drawing-room art of Davies had nothing in common, and the Impressionism of Prendergast was quite individual. The Eight had been swept together by Henri as a protest group. They were against the academic; representing a liberal rather than a new vision, they survived in art history as insurgents, dubbed the "Black

10

Gang" and the "Ash-can School." Sloan and Luks were the most important of the original eight; Henri was more significant as a teacher. George Bellows, pupil of Henri, was slightly younger but his powerful and dramatic art brought him quickly forward among the older men. He was a transitional figure who strove to assimilate the new influences from Europe. Like Bellows, Kenneth Hayes Miller also represented an early shift toward Modernism. He combined the subject-interest of the Eight with the new European conceptions of form. These were the frontiersmen of the new century in American art.

News from Abroad

The early American realists and reporters who shocked New York were contemporary with the *Fauves*, the "wild beasts" who were shocking Paris. Both groups attacked the academic, outraged the proprieties, brutalized familiar subtleties. There the resemblance ceased. The Eight, except for Prendergast, Davies and Glackens, were remote from European developments. They had observed with a fresh intensity, but they believed that reality was there before them to be caught on the wing, as though the painter were a good shot.

There is, however, another view of the artist's function based upon a less innocent philosophy. It is possible to think that we build up our reality through living, that we project concepts into our handiwork, and that this accretion of what was once thought is both the record and the thing recorded. This point of view has the disturbing power to endow material objects with qualities of spirit. A work of art then simply displays itself as a description of reality. It offers its color, its pattern, its style, which somehow correspond to the artist's emotions and to the temper of an epoch. Such a view implies that men are continuously constructing their spiritual house.

Artists who hold this view are dedicated men, of two species or temperaments. Some are excited primarily by the form or structure of a painting; they have a kinship with architects and are moved by mathematics and geometry. Others are primarily concerned with the emotional content. They are intent on projecting imagery as directly as possible, and the structure seems to them a mere vehicle. Such artists usually distort and exaggerate, using color and form for their psychological impact. And, since they probe their own emotions, they often give us the deeper responses of the subconscious mind—that dark continent which awaited discovery and exploration in our time.

The development of form and the projection of deep emotion were to become the two major interests of the first half of our century, and they were already well established in Europe during the first ten years. The *Fauves* led off with their venture in heightened emotionalism: Matisse, Derain, Braque, Vlaminck and Rouault had put Impressionism behind them and created an art out of the free rhythms and bold expressive color they had learned from Van Gogh and Gauguin. They exhibited in the first Autumn Salon, in 1903; and they dominated the Autumn Salon of 1905. It was there that the *Fauves* earned their name from critics and public.

A small group of Cézanne's paintings appeared in the Salon of 1905; another group followed the next year, and in 1907 there was a memorial exhibition of fifty-six of his canvases, for the painter had just died. Cézanne had lived so long in retirement in the south of France that he was scarcely known in Paris, but now his work won converts. His feeling for architecture—for organization in space—appealed to the deepest instincts of French painters. His discipline offered new rewards; little as his audience realized it, he had rediscovered the classic tradition.

During the opening years of the century a young and solitary Spaniard, Pablo Picasso, had been painting lonely and romantic canvases in Paris, awaiting the moment to rouse himself from his nostalgia. He now stepped forward and with apparent ease assumed a commanding position in the modern movement. Disdaining a choice between the classic organization of Cézanne and the violence of the *Fauves*, he appropriated both and bent them to his purposes. The *Fauves* had discovered Negro sculpture; its suave distortions offered them the force of the grotesque, but offered Picasso the strength of style.

Cézanne had generalized forms in terms of geometry, and Picasso took up where Cézanne left off. Between the exploration of space and sheer invention he discovered, or created, Cubism. It was a ten-year quest. Cubism and its abstract ramifications provided the sinews of organization and philosophy for the modern painter, and for the modern architect as well.

All Europe, the German, Italian and Russian painters—and eventually the whole world of art—responded to these changes. As always, there were Americans in Paris, and by now they were no longer there simply to learn to paint in France. They had come to share, and to add to their share, in an international undertaking. Maurice Prendergast knew Cézanne's painting as early as 1898, and he was the first to bring news of it to America. Alfred Maurer was in Paris by 1900; he became the first *Fauve* convert, although he was already an established conservative painter. Bernard Karfiol was in Paris in 1901; Max Weber was there by 1905. Charles Demuth, Arthur Dove, Marsden Hartley, Charles Sheeler, Thomas Benton and as many others followed along. Most of them stayed until they felt that they had gained something which they wished to offer America; some lingered indefinitely; others felt themselves overwhelmed and fled. But a change had come over them all. They had acquired a new consciousness of their profession.

Stieglitz

Two Americans played important roles as critics and sponsors of the modern movement, one in France, the other in America. In Paris, Gertrude Stein was one of the first to admire and buy the paintings of Cézanne, Picasso and Matisse, when these men were either unknown or despised. And she befriended the young Americans, Maurer, Demuth and Hartley. Her house was open to them; Hartley's letters to her as he traveled through Europe reveal the sustaining strength of her temperament.

In America, Alfred Stieglitz singled out the new men with the same sure instinct. He fostered the work of the American moderns, showing many of them in New York before they returned from abroad. These painters in general were more receptive personalities than the Eight, with less zeal for slugging it out with the public, and they needed someone to encourage and sustain them, to publish, advertise and sell them. They found their champion in Stieglitz, who was an artist in his own right as well as an impresario and dealer. He provided the spectacular, which the American public demanded and the artists lacked.

During his lifetime—he was eighty-one when he died in 1945—Stieglitz rediscovered photography, made it an art, and was never surpassed in his profession. In 1905 he founded the Photo-Secession Gallery, or "291 Fifth Avenue," which was soon to exhibit paintings as well as photographs. Since Stieglitz knew what photography was, he knew quite naturally what painting was not. In his gallery the photographer complemented the painter. In 1909 he gave Alfred Maurer his first American exhibition, and Marin and Hartley their first exhibitions anywhere. The following year he showed these painters, along with Arthur Dove and Max Weber; he gave Weber his first one-man show in 1911 and Dove the first in 1912. Georgia O'Keeffe was first shown in 1916 and again in 1917.

During these same years Stieglitz pioneered in introducing modern European art to America. He exhibited the paintings of Matisse and Rodin's water colors in 1908; Toulouse Lautrec's lithographs in 1909; Henri Rousseau's paintings and drawings and Cézanne's water colors in 1911, and Matisse's sculpture in 1912. In 1914 he gave the first one-man show for Brancusi, and the first exhibition of primitive Negro sculpture to be held in America.

It is this impressive list of events and dates that sets Stieglitz outside the time-lag in public reaction. He was aware of what went on in the world *when it happened*; he was an American Internationalist and his timing was right. This is the bare fact; but over and above the fact is an aura of the fabulous. He had P. T. Barnum's flair for a legend. He saw that the artist created a myth. His greatest *tour de force* was to Americanize the European influence. Those painters who were most steeped in current European

13

developments were brought forward as primeval Americans, and Stieglitz himself appeared in the guise of Walt Whitman. This was more than showmanship. Apparently he foresaw what American painting was to assimilate, thought of it as accomplished, and presented it as fact. By anticipating the future he helped to create it.

The Armory Show

The two streams of American art, the realistic reporters and the painters who had been influenced by Europe, came together in the Armory Show of 1913, where they poured down over the American public in a cataract. There were rapids and shoals ahead, but the Armory Show still marks the headwaters of navigation for modern American painting.

In the New York of 1910, apart from the small Madison Gallery and Alfred Stieglitz, there was hardly an outlet for the young advanced painters, and all about them was that easy collusion between the conservative painter and his subject, which seemed as interminable as Nature herself. A group of painters exhibiting at the Madison Gallery became fretful with stagnation and organized in December 1911 for the purpose of putting on a comprehensive show. Walt Kuhn, the leading spirit, went to see Arthur B. Davies, then one of the most influential figures in New York's world of art. Davies saw an opportunity to display not merely American painting but all the current achievements of Europe, which had reached the majority of American painters as rumor rather than experience. He stepped into the presidency of the Association of American Painters and Sculptors, as the organization was called, and completely changing the intention behind the exhibition, threw open the door to modern Europe. Kuhn meanwhile had solved the problem of a place for the show by engaging the 69th Armory on Lexington Avenue. There would be no limitation in scale.

In the summer of 1912, Davies sent Kuhn the catalogue of the Sonderbund Exhibition in Cologne, with the note: "I wish we could have a show like this." In response, Kuhn caught the next steamer and reached Germany as the exhibition was closing. He selected the works of artists whom he was seeing for the first time: Van Gogh, the Norwegian Munch, and the German sculptor Lehmbruck. He went on to the Hague where he had his first view of the work of Odilon Redon and arranged to give him a whole gallery in the exhibition. Improvising with assurance, he visited Munich and Berlin. Finally he went to Paris, where Alfred Maurer introduced him to the dealer Vollard, Walter Pach lent his aid, and the sculptor Jo Davidson took a hand. As the plans grew in scope Kuhn cabled for Davies to come over; he did so and the sacking of Paris went on apace. They went to London on the way home to see Roger Fry's second Grafton Gallery Show. In Paris, Walter Pach was left to bale and ship the European segment of the exhibition.

On the American side, the Association's members numbered twenty-five, and there were many other American exhibitors. Eleven of the names in the catalogue occur in this book: Luks, Sloan, Bellows, Kuhn, Kenneth Hayes Miller, Edward Hopper, Karfiol, Marin, Hartley, Charles Sheeler and Stuart Davis. These names themselves spell out the history of a period, but most of them were unknown at the time.

The Armory Show opened on February 17, 1913. Its preparation had by then become something of a family affair between artists, critics and collectors, all of whom were drawn together by their enthusiasm for doing something new. Divergencies of style, interest and taste ceased to be barriers; they became no more than the partitions between the galleries. Davies' taste was catholic and generous, and his statement of policy for the Association deserves to be recalled:

> This is not an institution but an association. It is composed of persons of varying tastes and predilections, who are agreed on one thing, that the time has arrived for giving the public here the opportunity to see for themselves the results of new influences at work in other countries in an art way.
>
> In getting together the work of the European Moderns, the Society has embarked on no controversy with any institution. Its sole object is to put the paintings, sculptures, and so on, on exhibition so that the intelligent may judge for themselves by themselves.
>
> Of course controversies may arise, just as they have arisen under similar circumstances in France, Italy, Germany and England. But they will not be the result of any stand taken by this Association as such; on the other hand we are perfectly willing to assume full responsibility for providing the opportunity to those who may take one side or the other.

The Pine Tree flag of the American Revolution was the exhibition's emblem, and all that was needed after that was the public. President Taft and the Governor and the Mayor of New York were invited to the opening and failed to appear; the public also stayed away for the first two weeks. Then the newspapers stumbled over the show, treating it as news rather than art, and the storm broke. Crowds arrived for their baptism of fire. The foreigners provided the shock: Cézanne and Van Gogh, Gauguin and Seurat were as strange as Brancusi and Matisse. Duchamps' *Nude Descending the Staircase* stole the show as the climax of the bizarre. Picasso was less to the fore—he is listed as Paul Picasso in the catalogue.

Caruso arrived and made caricatures; Theodore Roosevelt came on March 4th, the day that Woodrow Wilson was inaugurated, to see a world turned upside down, and recorded his impressions in the *Outlook*, providing the phrase "the lunatic fringe." The critics generally were aghast, with a few praiseworthy exceptions, notably Henry McBride. There were collectors who were wiser. Frank Crowninshield and Miss Lizzie P. Bliss came often and bought. John Quinn's purchases were the beginning of his

15

important collection; as a friend of Kuhn's he had agreed to serve as legal adviser to the Association, and he acquired a taste for the new. Bryson Burroughs persuaded the Metropolitan Museum to acquire a Cézanne. The show piled notoriety on top of achievement and commanded the presence both of its friends and its enemies. The portrait-painter Chase, who had not been invited to exhibit, walked silk-hatted and solitary through the galleries. The dignity of the Academy was at a discount. At the close of the show the jubilant painters paraded, led by the Armory's fife and drum.

The exhibition moved on to Chicago, where it was housed by the Art Institute. There the attendance was greater than it had been in New York. The Art Institute— today ablaze with a great collection of modern painting—was ill at ease, and the faculty of the Institute's school shepherded the pupils through, with explanations that were warnings much in the spirit of "crime does not pay." The director was quoted to the effect that "scarcely anybody took the more extreme parts of the exhibition seriously . . . even the art students, supposed to be very susceptible to passing influence, were not in the least affected."

Finally the show came to Boston, where it was presented by the Copley Society. The response there was more subdued, although Walt Kuhn remembered that "local psychoanalysts were especially vehement in their disapproval." And with that the Armory Show was over. The public had been amazed and shocked, but only the American painters themselves and a few far-sighted individuals were prepared to profit from their experience. American painters now lived in a larger world, and a difficult task of synthesis lay ahead.

Abstraction Comes Early

The older liberals of the Ash-can School, and the new painters who had responded to the European venture, had joined forces in the Armory Show to the discomfiture of academic art. But if these forces were joined they were not fused. The two trends remained distinct. They continued to represent two attitudes toward art—a literal over against a philosophic attitude—a native versus an international one. Something like a two-party system was established in American art, which, like American political parties, was based on geographical loyalties as well as an allegiance to ideas.

As with political parties, the two trends thereafter took turns in dominating art. The Armory Show was a revolutionary event; from that day on, the realists were no longer the vanguard, in spite of the fact that they still included such spectacular temperaments as Henri, Bellows, Luks and Sloan.

The change was not at once apparent. The First World War broke out in the year after the Armory Show; civilized contact with the rest of the world was blocked, and

16

the new artist lost what small share of public attention he had acquired. The academician might have thought that the danger was past. But the artist has a sensibility and an instinct for the special quality of his epoch—it is his business to bring it to light. From 1913 to the middle of the next decade a large number of America's best painters were working in an abstract manner. It was the first period of American abstract art. Max Weber, Joseph Stella, Charles Demuth, Andrew Dasburg, Stuart Davis, Karl Knaths, Preston Dickinson and Niles Spencer, to mention only outstanding names, were willing to learn from Cézanne and from Picasso, and they adapted Cubism to their requirements. Even the realistic Sheeler underwent the discipline of abstraction; and Georgia O'Keeffe painted a number of abstract canvases before she developed her decorative symbolical style.

But the American abstractionists never went to such logical lengths as the French Cubists; they compared to the Cubists as inventors compare to searchers in pure science. The pattern which they drew out of reality was not always geometric. The influence of Van Gogh and later German art invited a more emotional and personal expression, and a native romanticism never ceased to pulse through American painting. There is a flame-like quality, for instance, in the abstraction of Arthur Dove; and Morris Kantor, while drawing strength from German painting and aspects of Picasso, remains steeped in a romantic American mood. Stuart Davis came to abstraction slowly and has had a gradual and steady development; yet even his painting has never relaxed its hold on an underlying realism. Karl Knaths also is a painter who worked out a satisfactory and stable balance between realism and abstraction. Lyonel Feininger, an expatriate in those days, has continued to develop his own abstract style from the moment he discovered Cubism in 1912. Yet Feininger is far from a pure cubist; his art is a romantic composite. Finally, Marsden Hartley and John Marin, two major painters who loom large among the depictors of the American scene, are set apart from the literal by their early and persistent interest in the abstract.

The first period of American abstraction thus has a blurred pattern. It is a period which is too easily forgotten, now that abstraction has returned as a more popular art. And this is to some extent the fault of the older American painters themselves, for with few exceptions they put abstraction behind them in the course of time and turned to a more representative art. Most of the first generation of abstractionists were still in an early phase of their work, a phase primarily of importance for their future. Abstraction for them was a sort of discipline taken on for a purpose, rather than a way of life.

After a decade of this discipline, the best American painters had already resolved and absorbed their experience. They had matured and become simply individual painters about the time that a taste for the modern painting was becoming more general. The heyday of this interest in modern painting came in the twenties. Americans in mass had had a first-hand experience of Europe and our interest had been projected beyond the frontiers. Americans went abroad in peacetime armies. There was an entire American colony of painters and writers in Paris. European literature was making itself felt, along with European art. Proust and Joyce were the contemporary discoveries; a generation of American writers was impressed with the new depths plumbed in European writing.

Dos Passos and Hemingway, publishing in the twenties, had a new feeling for composing through association. Dos Passos, with his Camera Eye, was to create a mechanized stream of consciousness out of captions. Hemingway owed a debt to Gertrude Stein. T. S. Eliot, E. E. Cummings, Archibald MacLeish were using language in a new way. The very disillusionment of the period threw the writer back on style as an end in itself. Concentration, form, and subconscious imagery were now the preoccupation of writers as well as of painters. Post-war literature arrived as a powerful reinforcement for the artist.

But the writer had one great advantage over the painter. Since he wrote in English, European literature influenced him without competing for his audience. For the American artist, French painting was not only an influence, it was an active competitive commodity, and it was often pushed with a cool unconcern for real quality. American artists, when they organized the Armory Show and brought European art to America, were like the frogs in the fable. They had repudiated the dead log of the sovereign public, and they had brought in the stork which ate them up.

There was a reaction, and the painter was among the first to respond to a change of atmosphere. Naturalism in art, the regional, the homespun, began to gain allegiance. The grin of local pride supplanted the wrinkles of inquiry. The American painter felt that he had been tutored enough. And the change came quickly, before the business man had any inkling of the depression ahead, before the politician knew that he was to gamble on isolation.

New Museums

The depression struck in 1929. In that year and the following, New York witnessed the opening of two new museums dedicated primarily to the living artist. The Museum of Modern Art opened its doors in 1929, the Whitney Museum in 1931. These two institutions could hardly be expected to change the economic fate of the American painter, but they did provide the artist with honor and prestige at a crucial time. They were a sanctuary for his reputation, so that he did not fall into low esteem in the eyes of those who value success. The Museum of Modern Art embraced the whole modern field; the Whitney confined itself to American art. Both museums built on permanent collections of the recent past, and embarked on a program of frequent exhibitions of living artists. The Museums complemented each other.

The Whitney, although it was started later, had deeper roots in the past; it was the culmination of Mrs. Gertrude Vanderbilt Whitney's lifelong effort to assist the American artist. In 1908, the year of the Eight's sole exhibition, she had opened two galleries in her studio on Eighth Street. Here such painters as Sloan, Luks and Bellows had had a chance to show. The next step was the organization of the Whitney Studio Club in 1914, with twenty artist members. Here they exhibited, and the paintings purchased by Mrs. Whitney were destined to become the permanent collection of the Museum. The Club had grown to a membership of four hundred by 1928; it had become unwieldy by its very success, and its primary function of providing an outlet for new painters was no longer essential; there were now dealers anxious to show just such painters as the Club wished to advance. Accordingly, Mrs. Whitney's undertaking graduated into a museum: a private gesture had grown to a public benefaction. Through all these years the Whitney Galleries, the Club, and the Museum were under the directorship of the late Mrs. Juliana Force, whose personality gave the Museum its broad taste and its singleness of purpose. The Whitney has maintained a policy of frequent general exhibitions and has consistently sought out and welcomed unknown painters. And the writings of Lloyd Goodrich, the art historian, have added to the Museum's authority.

In the case of the Museum of Modern Art, earlier events also pointed the way. In 1920, Katherine S. Dreier, along with the French painter Marcel Duchamps, and the American photographer Man Ray, who had stayed on in Paris, founded the Société Anonyme. The Société's exhibitions were given over largely to contemporary European art of an abstract kind. Its activity underlined a public need, and touched the public spirit of the collectors of modern paintings.

The Museum of Modern Art was organized by a number of such public-spirited collectors who took note of the fact that "New York alone, of the great capitals of the world, lacks a public gallery where the founders and masters of the modern school can today be seen." The new museum was to present "the great modern painters— American and European—from Cézanne to the present day, but will be devoted primarily to living artists, with occasional homage to the masters of the nineteenth century." The Museum's first officers were A. Conger Goodyear, Miss Lizzie P. Bliss and Mrs. John D. Rockefeller, Jr.; and both Miss Bliss, through a spectacular bequest in 1931, and Mrs. Rockefeller, through sustained guidance and generous gifts, contributed greatly to the Museum's rapid growth.

The Museum is also fortunate in having had Alfred H. Barr, Jr., as its first director. He is still a guiding spirit, outstanding for his scholarship and his enthusiasm among all those who have recognized the artist, brought him before the public, and related him to his times.

During its first year, the Museum of Modern Art put on an exhibition of nineteen American painters. The list included a balanced representation of painters in the more factual American tradition—Sloan, Miller, Hopper, Burchfield, Kuhn, Speicher; those who had absorbed the European tradition—Demuth, Dickinson, Kuniyoshi, O'Keeffe, Sterne, Weber, Marin; the newly naturalized Pascin, and the American Feininger, who had worked most of his life in Germany, and whose abstract paintings were hardly known in this country. The exhibition proved how close the two schools had tended to grow, for the factual painters were now disciplined in structure, and the abstract painters hankered after subject-matter.

From time to time the Museum has signaled the maturity of a number of American painters by giving them major one-man shows. Even more significantly, it has put on group exhibitions of little-known Americans—as in 1942 and again in 1946—and given those painters prominence through its prestige. The majority of the painters so presented have justified the Museum's judgment and today stand in the foreground of the contemporary scene.

The American Scene

The reporters and realists had not remained idle since the days of the Eight. A number of painters of scale and power followed George Bellows. Guy Pène duBois made large concessions to simplification and structure; Eugene Speicher painted massive romantic portraits, overlaying sculptural figures with a patina of color. But there is less freshness in this direction, for the studio and the art colony bred monotony of subject and style. A newer impulse came from Edward Hopper and Charles Burch-field, who gave an intense and specific accounting of the world they knew. Hopper described New York and New England; Burchfield reported on Ohio and upper New York; yet both of these painters foreshadowed a change. There was something more reflective, more inward, in their vision. Burchfield is a painter of imagination, Hopper of mood.

Charles Sheeler was a reporter who clung to the exact visual world with his camera. He was absorbed in photography; yet what he gave us in his paintings of factories and industrial scenes and of Pennsylvania houses was not so much the object as an optical experience. Sheeler possessed a micrometer vision capable of taking the measure of an industrial age. Reginald Marsh continued the racy account of the life of New York City begun in the work of John Sloan. Marsh studied with Sloan, and he is closest in mood to the early reporters.

Then, in the early thirties, three midwestern painters impinged on the national consciousness, producing paintings and offering personal histories that perfectly illus, trated the re,publicized American theme. Thomas Benton, John Steuart Curry and Grant Wood were dissimilar, but they were properly grouped in the public's imagina, tion. All three had a feeling for scale, for drama, for working in a major key. All three painted a legend and were able to identify themselves with it. It was part of this legend that they were humble men from the country who had gone to Europe to learn to paint and had escaped in time from the engulfing decadence to redeem themselves in the pure air of home. They did not report on the life of the midwest as Sloan had once reported on the life of New York. They depicted a myth, built out of types or typical scenes which already existed in the popular imagination and merely had to be recognized. Such an art taps immediate sources of power, but it soon becomes sterile. All three painters began with emphatic statements that have an important place in the history of American art. All three sank on occasion to the level of book,jacket makers, while there was no lack of historians to write the blurb. All three painters set a style; the arabesques of Benton, the archaic precision of Wood, the romantic tableaux of Curry provided a vocabulary that scores of other painters adopted with more or less success.

It is important to note that the art which had returned to favor was the only one the New Deal could have spread through the public buildings of the country. By some foresight, also, the painters had scattered across the land, decentralizing the new forces in art. Regional schools were springing up in the midwest, in Chicago and in Cleve, land, at the very moment when the New York market was growing lean. The thirties were the years of the American Scene.

Government in Art

The Federal Government under the New Deal launched two separate projects to help the artists. The first employed the best talents to decorate public buildings. The second undertook to provide work for artists as artisans, lest a cultural drought follow the economic. For a short while, both of these functions were part of the Public Works of Art Project, organized through the initiative of Edward Bruce. In 1935, Bruce was transferred to a newly formed Section of Fine Arts under the Treasury Department, and government assistance for the artist was reorganized as the Federal Arts Project under the WPA. Holger Cahill, who became the national head, was only empowered to employ those artists who were already on relief. At one time the Project employed some five thousand artists, nearly half of whom were engaged creatively. They produced murals, posters and a visual record of American artifacts—the Index of American

Design. The Project circulated exhibitions and subsidized the artist in his home territory, striving to decentralize art and artist and undo the concentration of art in New York. Culturally, its achievement was invaluable in salvaging a generation with a bent for artistic expression; but it was a political liability, and was blindly surrendered as a superfluous liberal outpost in 1939.

With the coming of the war, the hope that the artist might share directly in the national effort was revived. Propaganda, the press and history had their claims, and patriotism was in a generous mood. An Army program for artists in the field was accordingly organized; it was well conceived and the artists were well chosen. Nevertheless, it died a quick death in Congress. The magazine *Life* took over the program entire, and so the result was much the same; the war was recorded and the results displayed. The Navy, more cautious than the Army, had a limited art program which did survive.

Finally, in 1946, the State Department found itself by accident patronizing the American artist. It purchased a group of paintings presumably to influence other nations, and the paintings were sent on a good-will tour as a cultural gesture. They had traveled to South America, and were already in Europe before the least responsible section of the American press realized its opportunity and howled its contempt in the taxpayers' name. Congress turned critic and the State Department canceled the tour, eventually selling the paintings to museums at a profit.

Social Comment

By the thirties, even the most factual painters had achieved a more personal vision. The journalists of the first decade of the century had been reporters; the journalists of the thirties were editorialists; consciously or not, opinion, judgment and belief colored their work. Paintings were charged with pity or political faith; the same emotion turned the artist to satire when the subject was unsympathetic. It was a decade of liberal hope.

Propaganda is a legitimate challenge to the artist. But propaganda does not necessarily demand the means which art demands since it does not insist on pictorial means for a pictorial result. Also it offers an emotional satisfaction in itself, one that is too often substituted for the satisfactions of art.

If there is to be ethical judgment—in other words a message—the painter must offer explicit subject-matter. He can hardly be abstract. On the other hand, he can and does force his comment by exaggeration, often falling into the tradition, wittingly or not, of the American political cartoon. But the influence on which the recent painter of propaganda has most frequently drawn is German Expressionism. Modern German art was steeped in moral indignation—or rather it was steeped in animosities which appeared as moral indignation, for one cannot hate without justification. Surrender to the negative emotion of hatred is the great liability of propaganda art.

There is a further liability: the propagandist, in our doctrinaire days, tends to deal in principles and generalizations. He is thus led to substitute types for individuals—which is one of the weaknesses of our times.

The artists who have escaped these hazards have given us some of the best canvases painted in America. They have been able to create a personal language whose meaning is plain. At their best, they have known how to compress general concepts into concrete forms, how to personify passions, how to see all humanity in a single human being. They have used pity not to cloud vision but to sharpen it; they have refined the sense of tragedy, and made men pause and look where none paused before.

Ben Shahn and Jack Levine are the strongest of these painters. In their painting, the pre-depression world is quite lost in time past. The symbol is explicit, exaggeration underlines intention, simplification serves the composition as well as the drama. In a different vein, but with the same intent, Peter Blume's brilliant and complex art combines social comment with the precise vision of a Sheeler. William Gropper, Aaron Bohrod, Raphael Soyer, Joseph Hirsch, George Grosz, Mitchell Siporin, Philip Evergood and Robert Gwathmey have all added to the dignity and depth of American art. In a time of brutality, there is no need to apologize for compassion. A sense of the tragic, of human fate, does not produce art, but it tests art by its own seriousness.

Later Abstraction

Perhaps it was the war which ran representation into the ground. There was a dazzling mechanical display; there was a colossal human-interest story. It was journalism's opportunity, but somehow it seemed to surfeit the artist with journalism. War does not ask for individuals; it asks for types. It demands type reactions. Americans, pressed into type form and furnished with type emotions, began to place a higher evaluation on individuality, and no one did this more than the artist.

With the coming of peace, the painters once more returned to making paintings which dealt with concepts and with states of mind. Abstraction revived—or more precisely, a second period of abstract painting now set in. Fluid, complex and eclectic it often made the earlier abstraction seem preliminary and unwieldy. It offered variety, not only through eclecticism, but because so many painters were taking a hand in it—it was a popular movement. In the first abstract period Cubism was modified by

Expressionism; in the second, Expressionism was generally replaced by an admixture of surrealist symbols. Free association took the place of exaggeration as a means of recording emotion.

A few painters, Feininger, Davis and Knaths, bridge over from the first abstract period to the current one. Among these, Lyonel Feininger is the most imposing, with his atmospheric cubism created out of controlled light. Stuart Davis paints abstract synopses of experience that are as uncompromising in color as billboards—they have a crisp American tang. Milton Avery—to stay with the older, more familiar names— is more abstract in his color than in his forms. Tamayo and Rattner are bolder; the former is more expressive than abstract, like all Mexicans; the latter has lived long in Paris, and draws on Picasso for his abstract forms, on Rouault for his human or moral interest.

The new abstraction took more from Europe than from the earlier American abstract period. In Europe there had been no major return to realism such as broke the trend in America. Instead, representation had been put at the service of inquiry, or had been used to illustrate subconscious imagery by the Surrealists. At the same time, abstraction had become mechanized in the painting of Ozenfant, Corbusier and Leger, and it had reached its most architectural form in the compositions of the Dutch precisionist, Mondrian. In contrast to Mondrian's suppressed constructions, the brilliant amorphous designs of the Spanish painter Miro hover between abstraction and Surrealism, and evoke, or mock, organic forms. The range from Mondrian to Miro is very great; both have had enormous influence. Mondrian has probably had more impact on the decorative arts than on painting itself; whereas Miro has excited many younger painters, who skirt the dangers of fluid and facile decoration.

In the new American abstract period Adolph Gottlieb, Baziotes, Stamos and Byron Browne, to mention a few among many, have a fluid, organic, non-architectural form of abstraction; they conceive a world of cells as seen in the eye of the microscope, of hieroglyphics and symbols. I. Rice Pereira, on the contrary, has a highly geometric and mechanized art. Loren MacIver can turn from one extreme to the other; so can Rico Lebrun, who moves from Surrealism to geometry, and who occasionally communicates in the clear, in strong realistic terms. Philip Guston has the same pliability. Morris Graves has evolved an oriental mysticism, narrow in range, which is dependent entirely on symbols.

The interest in Surrealism and abstraction was brought to focus in a major exhibition held in 1947 by the Chicago Art Institute. The vast majority of American painters found themselves close enough to the abstract movement to take part. But that very fact points to a new versatility and the growing individuality of the American artist. He is no longer wedded to a school.

24

Romanticism and the Individual

American painting has always had a substratum of romanticism; it becomes romantic automatically whenever it ceases to be something else. Henry Mattson and Franklin Watkins follow in the native romantic genealogy; they are related to Ryder. Milton Avery has a romantic mood which abstraction fails to disguise and the same could be said for even more abstract painters, such as Guston or MacIver. Karfiol's painting, which began with a silvery nostalgia and advanced to a colorful sensuality, is romantic at all times; Maurice Sterne is richly romantic, regardless of the style on the surface. Kuniyoshi has an urban sophisticated romanticism. There are romantics who are gay, such as Doris Lee; who are exuberant, such as Corbino; and there are mournful literary romantics, like Albright. Alexander Brook is an accomplished romantic realist. However much they all differ among themselves, they also differ as a group from the Neo-Romantics who came out of France in the late twenties.

Neo-Romanticism was exotic and Parisian in a fashionable sense; it required a sensitive and sophisticated audience. It would not lend itself, one might have supposed, to transplanting. Yet two of its painters, Eugene Berman and Pavel Tchelitchew, have survived and thrived in America. Both have great brilliance and technical skill, and a certain hardihood and resourcefulness which sustains their sensibility. They are supremely decorative, and both have designed for the theater and the ballet. They know how to mix subconscious imagery with decoration so that Surrealism no longer shocks and the decoration escapes vacuity. Of the Americans influenced by the Neo-Romantics, Stuempfig appears to be the most significant for the future; he has been able to lift his moving nostalgia into a major key.

The painting of Karl Zerbe is essentially romantic in mood; his skill and sophistication place him close to the Neo-Romantics, in spite of his deeper, more emotional subject-matter.

Meanwhile a handful of primitives, Eilshemius, Kane, Hirschfield and Pippin among them, have painted with timeless detachment during this half-century. The spontaneous art of these hardy individuals is also close to the romantic mood. By definition, they are not a movement; but with their charm and appeal they have invited imitation and their innocence has often been counterfeited.

Once one begins to see American painters as romantics, more and more names crowd in. The painters of the American scene are romantics too; the "social comment" painters give us romantic scenes, even if they have a somber meaning, and even the abstract painters have an increasingly emotional bias. The basic romantic character of American painting comes through as the one changeless aspect of American art in the last fifty years.

The Modern movement then, has been an overlying experience, a discipline in structure and in ideas. Discipline is, or should be, a surrender of freedom in order to gain more freedom, an acceptance of classification in order to outgrow it and win through to individuality. Such a process appears to have been gradually taking place. The persistent romantic trend, the diverse eclecticism, suggest that painters are testing out new freedoms and have less allegiance to theory, and that the whole period is taking on historical perspective.

The development of individuality is the most significant factor at the present moment, a sign of maturity, and the best harbinger of the time to come.

General Bibliography

America & Alfred Stieglitz: A Collective Portrait (edited by Waldo Frank, Lewis Mumford, Dorothy Norman, Paul Rosenfeld and Harold Rugg), New York, 1934.

Anderson Gallery: *The Forum Exhibition of Modern American Painters* (with a foreword by Alfred Stieglitz), New York, 1916.

Art in America in Modern Times (edited by Alfred H. Barr, Jr., and Holger Cahill), New York, 1934.

Association of American Painters and Sculptors, Inc.: *International Exhibition of Modern Art* (preface by Frederick James Gregg which includes the statement by Arthur B. Davies, president of the association), New York, 1913.

Boswell, Peyton, Jr.: *Modern American Painting*, New York, 1939.

Brooklyn Museum: *The Eight* (with a foreword by John I. H. Baur and "Recollections" by Everett Shinn), Brooklyn, New York, 1944.

Carnegie Institute, Department of Fine Arts: *Survey of American Painting*, Pittsburgh, 1940.

Cheney, Sheldon: *A Primer of Modern Art*, New York, 1924.

Janis, Sidney: *They Taught Themselves: American Primitive Painters of the 20th Century*, New York, 1942.

Kootz, Samuel M.: *Modern American Painters*, Norwood, Massachusetts, 1930.

Kootz, Samuel M.: *New Frontiers in American Painting*, New York, 1943.

Kuhn, Walt: *The Story of the Armory Show*, New York, 1938.

Landgren, Marchal E.: *Years of Art: The Story of the Art Students' League of New York* (with an introduction by Walter Pach), New York, 1940.

Museum of Modern Art: *Paintings by Nineteen Living Americans*, New York, 1930.

Museum of Modern Art: *American Painting and Sculpture, 1862–1932* (with an essay by Holger Cahill), New York, 1932.

Museum of Modern Art: *Americans 1942: 18 Artists from 9 States* (edited by Dorothy C. Miller), New York, 1942.

Museum of Modern Art: *Romantic Painting in America* (edited by James Thrall Soby and Dorothy C. Miller), New York, 1943.

Museum of Modern Art: *American Realists and Magic Realists* (edited by Alfred H. Barr, Jr., and Dorothy C. Miller, with statements by the artists and an introduction by Lincoln Kirstein), New York, 1943.

Museum of Modern Art: *Fourteen Americans* (edited by Dorothy C. Miller, with statements by the artists and others), New York, 1946.

Newark Museum: *American Primitives* (with an essay by Holger Cahill), Newark, New Jersey, 1930.

Philadelphia Museum of Art: *Artists of the Philadelphia Press, William Glackens, George Luks, Everett Shinn, John Sloan*, Philadelphia, 1945.

Phillips, Duncan: *A Collection in the Making*, New York and Washington, D.C., 1926.

Phillips, Duncan: *The Artist Sees Differently*, 2 vols., New York and Washington, D.C., 1931.

Richardson, Edgar P.: *American Romantic Painting* (edited by Robert Freund), New York, 1944.

Romanticism in America (edited by George Boas), Baltimore, Maryland, 1940.

Whitney Museum of American Art: *New York Realists, 1900–1914* (with an essay by Helen Appleton Read), New York, 1937.

Whitney Museum of American Art: *20th Century Artists; Painting, Sculpture and Graphic Arts from the Permanent Collection of the Whitney Museum of American Art*, New York, 1939.

Whitney Museum of American Art: *Pioneers of Modern Art in America* (with an essay by Lloyd Goodrich), New York, 1946.

Note: Thanks are due the Museum of Modern Art for special permission to quote from *Fourteen Americans* edited by Dorothy C. Miller (in "Loren MacIver"), from *Charles Sheeler* by William Carlos Williams (in "Charles Sheeler"), and from *Americans 1942*, edited by Dorothy C. Miller (in "Joseph Hirsch").

List of Painters and Paintings

1. GEORGE LUKS
   The Spielers, 1905. Oil, 36×26
   Present Owner: The Addison Gallery of American Art, Andover,
      Massachusetts

2. JOHN SLOAN
   McSorley's Bar, 1912. Oil, 26×32
   Present Owner: The Detroit Institute of Arts

3. GEORGE BELLOWS
   Stag at Sharkey's, 1907. Oil, 36×48
   Present Owner: The Cleveland Museum of Art

4. KENNETH HAYES MILLER
   The Shopper, 1928. Oil, 41×33
   Present Owner: The Whitney Museum of American Art, New York

5. WALT KUHN
   The Blue Clown, 1931. Oil, 30×25
   Present Owner: The Whitney Museum of American Art, New York

*6. ARTHUR G. DOVE
   Sand Barge, 1930. Oil on beaverboard, 30×40
   Present Owner: The Phillips Gallery, Washington

*7. CHARLES DEMUTH
   My Egypt, 1925. Oil, 36×30
   Present Owner: The Whitney Museum of American Art, New York

8. PRESTON DICKINSON
   Old Quarter, Quebec, 1927. Oil, 24×30
   Present Owner: The Phillips Gallery, Washington

9. MAX WEBER
   Whither Now? 1939. Oil, 60×40
   Present Owner: A. P. Rosenberg & Company, New York

*10. LYONEL FEININGER
   Glorious Victory of the Sloop "Maria," 1926. Oil, $21\frac{1}{2}×33\frac{1}{2}$
   Present Owner: The City Art Museum of St. Louis

11. MORRIS KANTOR
   Farewell to Union Square, 1931. Oil, 36×27
   Present Owner: The Newark Museum, Newark, New Jersey

Notes: All paintings are reproduced in this volume.
   An asterisk (*) before a title indicates that the painting is reproduced in color.
   "Oil" denotes Oil on Canvas.
   Measurements are to the nearest half-inch, height preceding width.

12. JOHN MARIN
    Deer Isle, Boats, and Pertaining Thereto, 1927.   Water color, $17\frac{1}{2} \times 22\frac{1}{2}$
    Present Owner: Keith Warner, Esq., Fort Lauderdale, Florida

13. KARL KNATHS
    Maritime, 1931.   Oil, 40×32
    Present Owner: The Phillips Gallery, Washington

14. CHARLES SHEELER
    Upper Deck, 1929.   Oil, $29\frac{1}{2} \times 22\frac{1}{2}$
    Present Owner: The Fogg Museum of Art, Harvard University

*15. MARSDEN HARTLEY
    Fox Island, Maine, 1937–38.   Oil, $21\frac{1}{2} \times 28$
    Present Owner: The Addison Gallery of American Art, Andover,
    Massachusetts

*16. STUART DAVIS
    Red Cart, 1932.   Oil, 32×50
    Present Owner: The Addison Gallery of American Art, Andover,
    Massachusetts

17. EDWARD HOPPER
    Dawn in Pennsylvania, 1942.   Oil, 32×52
    Present Owners: Mr. and Mrs. Otto Spaeth, New York

18. CHARLES BURCHFIELD
    November Evening, 1934.   Oil, 32×52
    Present Owner: The Metropolitan Museum of Art, New York

19. REGINALD MARSH
    Why not use the "L"?, 1930.   Tempera on panel, 36×48
    Present Owner: The Whitney Museum of American Art, New York

20. THOMAS HART BENTON
    Cattle Loading, West Texas, 1930.   Oil, 18×38
    Present Owner: The Addison Gallery of American Art, Andover,
    Massachusetts

21. GRANT WOOD
    American Gothic, 1930.   Oil on masonite, 30×25
    Present Owner: The Art Institute of Chicago

22. JOHN STEUART CURRY
    Baptism in Kansas, 1925.   Oil, 40×50
    Present Owner: The Whitney Museum of American Art, New York

23. BEN SHAHN
    Fourth of July Orator, 1943.   Tempera, 22×30
    Present Owner: James Thrall Soby, Esq., Farmington, Connecticut

24. WILLIAM GROPPER
    Isolationist.   Oil, $20 \times 16\frac{1}{2}$
    Present Owners: Robert and Joyce K. Rosenberg, White Plains, New York

*25. MITCHELL SIPORIN
      Dream of the Good Life, 1941.   Gouache, 24×34
      Present Owner: The Downtown Gallery, New York

*26. ABRAHAM RATTNER
      April Showers, 1939.   Oil, 32×39½
      Present Owners: Mr. and Mrs. Roy R. Neuberger, New York

27.   GEORGE GROSZ
      No Let Up, 1940.   Oil, 29×21
      Present Owners: Mr. and Mrs. Frederick B. Adams, Jr., New York

28.   JACK LEVINE
      String Quartette, 1934–37.   Tempera and oil on masonite.
      Present Owner: The Metropolitan Museum of Art, New York

29.   JOSEPH HIRSCH
      Portrait of an Old Man, 1939.   Oil, 44×30
      Present Owner: The Museum of Fine Arts, Boston

30.   AARON BOHROD
      Landscape near Chicago, 1934.   Oil on prestwood, 24×32
      Present Owner: The Whitney Museum of Modern Art, New York

*31. MILTON AVERY
      Music Maker, 1946.   Oil, 40×32
      Present Owner: Durand-Ruel, Inc., New York

*32. HYMAN BLOOM
      Buried Treasure, 1948.   Oil, 43×43
      Present Owner: Durlacher Brothers, New York

33.   PETER BLUME
      South of Scranton, 1931.   Oil, 56×66
      Present Owner: The Metropolitan Museum of Art, New York

34.   RICO LEBRUN
      Vertical Composition, 1945.   Oil, 70×32
      Present Owners: Mr. and Mrs. George Dangerfield, New York

35.   LOREN MACIVER
      The Sidewalk, 1940.   Oil, 40×32
      Present Owner: The Addison Gallery of American Art, Andover,
      Massachusetts

36.   I. RICE PEREIRA
      Green Depth, 1944.   Oil, 31×42
      Present Owner: The Metropolitan Museum of Art, New York

*37. ADOLPH GOTTLIEB
      Pictograph, 1942.   Oil, 48×36
      Present Owner: Jaques Seligmann & Company, New York

38. MORRIS GRAVES
   Journey, 1944.   Tempera, 26 × 30
   Present Owner: Benjamin Baldwin, Esq., New York

39. BERNARD KARFIOL
   Boy, ca. 1925.   Oil, 36 × 27
   Present Owner: The Phillips Gallery, Washington

40. HENRY E. MATTSON
   Wings of the Morning, 1937.   Oil, 36 × 50
   Present Owner: The Metropolitan Museum of Art, New York

41. FRANKLIN C. WATKINS
   Fire Eater, 1933–34.   Oil, 60 × 39
   Present Owner: The Philadelphia Museum of Art

42. YASUO KUNIYOSHI
   Bouquet and Stove, 1929.   Oil, 65 × 40
   Present Owner: The Artist

43. PAVEL TCHELITCHEW
   Fish Bowl, 1938.   Gouache, 21 × 18
   Present Owner: Durlacher Brothers, New York

*44. EUGENE BERMAN
   Paludes, 1937.   Oil, 32 × 46
   Present Owner: M. Knoedler & Company, New York

*45. WALTER STUEMPFIG, JR.
   Two Houses, 1946.   Oil, 25 × 30
   Present Owner: The Corcoran Gallery of Art, Washington

46. KARL ZERBE
   St. Louis Drawing Room, 1946.   Encaustic, 40 × 34
   Present Owner: The Artist

47. LOUIS EILSHEMIUS
   Contentment, 1903.   Oil, 30 × 20
   Present Owner: C. H. Kleeman, Esq., New York

48. JOHN KANE
   Prosperity's Increase, 1933.   Oil
   Present Owner: William S. Paley, Esq., New York

49. MORRIS HIRSCHFIELD
   Nude at the Window, 1941.   Oil, 54 × 30
   Present Owner: M. Martin Janis, Esq., Buffalo

50. HORACE PIPPIN
   Holy Mountain, II, 1944.   Oil, $21\frac{1}{2} × 29\frac{1}{2}$
   Present Owner: Edward A. Bragaline, Esq., New York

The Painters

George Luks: 1867-1933

George Luks, along with John Sloan, began his career working on the *Philadelphia Press,* as one of a group of illustrators turned painter. The group was associated with Robert Henri, who taught at the Pennsylvania Academy of Fine Arts. The young men were the radicals of their day—it was the turn of the century—but their radicalism was defiance of the academic and conventional; it antedated the revolution in modern painting. These radicals were the nucleus of a protest group, "The Eight," and it is largely the result of Luks' influence that they were called the "Ash-can School."

Luks became staff artist for the old *New York World,* and like Sloan he painted the life of the city, and the haunts and pleasures of O. Henry's *Four Million.* He was a painter content with summary and striking effects, and he handled a brush with gusto. His canvases tend to be sketchy and incomplete, unless his subjects, which often have a Dickensian relish and roguery about them, come to his assistance and fill the frames with their warmth and vitality.

There was a fabulous buffoonery about Luks. It was his histrionic pleasure to pass himself off for famous characters in saloons, to provoke fights and stand aside to watch the outcome, and to make a welsh rabbit over the gas jet in Henri's studio, mounted on a chair on a table. He denied that Henri influenced his painting. "The world never had but two artists," he said, "Frans Hals and little old George Luks."

Luks painted on into the Modern movement, which presented a formidable problem to men who had been the revolutionaries before the Armory Show of 1913. The show acquainted America with the current developments in Europe and it was thereafter no longer enough to be colorful and strident. Luks' painting grew self-conscious, he strengthened and simplified his forms, and his painting both gained and lost as it grew more deliberate. Yet his best canvases are the fortunate, spontaneous flights, sustained by a sense of drama shared by the subject and the painter. These canvases still convey just what he intended: that certain anonymous people were full of the fire of life at a now lost moment in time.

1. The Spielers, 1905

1

John Sloan: 1871-

John Sloan offers the best comparison between the realistic reporters and the painters who were to come after them, for there is a long overlap in time: Sloan, the last important painter of the radical "Eight," is still living. Of all the painters of the so-called Ash-can School, he gives us the clearest record of his epoch, for he is a born genre painter. He painted New York, the waterfront, the bar, the fire-escape, and the rooftop, the theater, the playground, the vacant lot that is so full of life. He takes us on a night prowl through the city. He painted an indelible portrait of Washington Square. There is a full painterly quality in his work which makes little canvases big. He is not caught in trivialities: color and light flood areas to which they are assigned. His painting is always animated: there are Sloan nudes; there are no Sloan still-lifes.

John Sloan grew up in Philadelphia, and was responsible for the support of his family when he was only sixteen. He worked for a bookseller, and studied at night. He became an artist-journalist working for the *Philadelphia Inquirer* and for the Press; later he shifted to the *New York Herald* and became an illustrator for the *Century, McClure's, Collier's* and *Everybody's*. But the colorful old *Masses*, of which he was art editor, proved to be the right outlet for his sympathies and his talents. His many etchings, which are excellent, and his lithographs carry the load of an extraordinary documentation.

Sloan was a crusader even more than his fellow-recorders. He was a battler for decency and justice in society. He fought for his profession; he helped in the organization of the Armory Show; he was the president of the Independents for many years. More responsive to life than to conceptions, he throve on battle, and like an old soldier he has lived on to a time when men have less high hearts and give him a perfunctory loyalty.

2. McSorley's Bar, 1912

George Bellows: 1882-1925

George Wesley Bellows was the perfect embodiment of the American realist's robust ideal: a direct, forthright man with abounding self-confidence and the talent to back it up. Even in his twenties he was self-supporting as a painter; he had an instinct for leadership and his paint conveyed his vitality. His subjects are set in a spotlight glare and his values are melodramatic. Bellows had been a baseball player, and liked athletic clubs and arenas, and he made the prizefight subject his own. The *Stag at Sharkey's*, painted in 1908, was one of his spectacular early performances. If the paint is forced, the masculinity in his art is genuine and convincing; all through his painting he has a man's response to men, women and children and to human endeavor.

He never went abroad and he made a virtue of it, but the challenge of the School of Paris, when it reached him, was something which he had to take up. He had won the battle over the direct use of paint, and he entered the battle of aesthetic theory with an athlete's confidence. He did not realize that his strength lay in a baroque sense of movement, violence and flow which kept pace with his feeling for intense contrasts. As a theorist he mistook rigidity for structure, and he put his figures in splints. He subscribed to a nostrum called Dynamic Symmetry, and pondered on elaborate triangulations and centered compositions in the "dominant eye." His talents survived his experiments; there were times when they seemed to triumph in spite of him, when complex design and spontaneous feeling fused, when he was painter of both life and ideas.

He died suddenly of appendicitis at the age of forty-three, and doubtless because of his early death his canvases have a transitional quality. Yet he saw the problem, and the opportunity, with which his generation was confronted. He did succeed in building his best paintings on an abstract or architectural base, and they are filled with a disciplined and controlled power.

3. Stag at Sharkey's, 1907

Kenneth Hayes Miller: 1876-

Like Henri, Kenneth Hayes Miller is one of America's important painter-teachers, and his canvases are not his sole accomplishment. This is not to underestimate him as a painter; it is to add something further to his credit. He began his teaching career in 1899 at the New York School of Art and has taught at the Art Students' League since 1911. Thus his influence dates from the very beginning of the century.

Miller was only eleven years younger than Henri, and six years older than Bellows, but in his mature painting he comes far closer to modern times. He is not concerned with brushwork, that is to say with surface characteristics. His interest is in form, and his own paintings are clearly conceptions and not renderings of the scene before him. He sets three-dimensional volumes in space and he has a feeling for clear delicate color.

It is Miller's subject-matter that reminds us of his generation. His tired women shoppers on Fourteenth Street lack the individuality which Sloan would have given them, but that was not what absorbed Miller. Grandeur of composition was his aim; with a certain irony he sets the monumental design over against the commonplace chore of living. This is imposing when it succeeds; but he confines himself to monotonous types, and what should have been timeless often sags with the inertia of the subject.

Miller's painting corresponds to a transitional phase in the work of Renoir, when the French painter found fault with the flimsiness of Impressionism and set himself to study form. For a while Renoir painted plastic—almost plaster—monuments over which his delicate color was somewhat incongruously dappled; later on his color and his new-found forms were to fuse into masterpieces, but Miller does not enter this promised land, and his color always remains an application to the formal concept.

He looms up large, however, when set against his contemporaries. To build paintings with a rigorous concern for structure was something new. What was difficult for one generation came more naturally to the next. And that brings us around again to Miller's further accomplishment; his influence as a teacher of the younger men.

4. The Shopper, 1928

40

4

Walt Kuhn: 1880-

The absence of formal training may have helped Walt Kuhn escape the transitional quality that marks the work of so many painters of this generation. Before he was twenty he was a cartoonist on a San Francisco paper. Later he travelled in France, Germany, Holland and Spain. He looked with a discerning glance on the contemporary movements; as a critic he understood what was going on about him, and his work in assembling the Armory Show was proof of his wise appraisal of the times. And he was a valued adviser of Lizzie P. Bliss and John Quinn, the collectors.

Kuhn's painting assimilated the influences of Cézanne, Manet and Derain. The resultant style he pared down to its simplest elements; there is a dynamism and directness in his work that puts an American stamp upon it. One conceives him to be a man of action who sees painting as a social activity rather than a spiritual quest.

It is primarily Kuhn's relation to subject-matter which marks him as a painter of an earlier generation and relates him to Henri and Luks. There are no moral generalizations; the model for Kuhn is simply a target. When he gives us a striking procession of figures from the circus or burlesque show, he is concerned with direct impact: of subject on painter, and of painter on audience. He was absorbed by the circus and by ballet, since they too hold an audience through color and form.

Kuhn's *Blue Clown* is one of the most effective of his canvases. The painter does not set himself apart from his model, but gladly joins forces with him in arresting the eye.

5. The Blue Clown, 1931

5

Arthur G. Dove: 1880-1946

Arthur G. Dove had a precocious talent; at the age of nine he was already studying painting in Geneva, New York. There is a correspondence between this precocity and the advanced place he constantly occupied in the whole Modern movement in America. He was among the early abstractionists, exhibiting with Alfred Stieglitz in 1910. During the next decade, while many of the most important American painters were working in abstract terms derived from Cubism, Dove, an exception, veered away from this architectural interest and developed forms which were fluid and rhythmic. At the same time his use of color was quite personal. He built compositions out of the local colors of objects, which he termed their "condition of light." This fluid, organic, non-architectural painting is much nearer to the second and current abstract period in American art than it is to the work of Dove's contemporaries. Thus he is not only one of America's earliest abstract painters, but he stands comparison with the most recent.

But Dove's achievement, remarkable though it was in its time, is restricted in scale and range. Lacking the power to load transcendent emotion into abstract forms, he tends toward the decorative, and stirs only a rarefied aesthetic response.

After graduation from Cornell College in his native region, he worked as an illustrator. In 1908, he went abroad, but returned, in 1912–18, to Connecticut, then for a while to a houseboat in the Harlem River, and finally to upstate New York.

6. Sand Barge, 1930

9

Charles Demuth: 1883-1935

Charles Demuth had a tenuous yet distinct genius—a genius for which the perfect medium was water color. Painting as a transcript of emotion, and Cubism—the two poles of the modern movement—both attracted him. His elegant linear style was adapted to both. When Demuth illustrated Henry James' *Turn of the Screw* and *The Beast in the Jungle*, he distilled out of James those qualities which forecast the twentieth century: the feeling for organization, the scorn of the accidental, the response to the promptings of the subconscious mind.

In his architectural paintings Demuth jostled buildings together to suit his plan. They might be colonial churches, or as modern as grain elevators and factories. The skies were carved by interlocking bands of light until they too became architecture. Often they were the most authoritative part of the picture, for man's laws are haphazard, but those of nature are fixed. *My Egypt* is a masterpiece of this kind.

Finally there are Demuth's flower and fruit still-lifes; these are pure and crystalline, at once distinguished and preserved, for the fruit is to be seen and not tasted and the flowers have no scent.

Demuth's own life corresponded to the detachment in his art: there is little to record. He studied at the Pennsylvania Academy under Thomas Anshutz, had a year abroad in 1907, and made subsequent trips before and after the First World War. He first appeared in Stieglitz's group in 1925. In all, Stieglitz gave Demuth three one-man shows. Demuth lived and painted in New York and in his home town of Lancaster, Pennsylvania to which he returned in uncertain health about 1921. His factory scenes are taken from nearby Coatesville, Pennsylvania, and he painted for several seasons at Provincetown on Cape Cod.

7. My Egypt, 1925

7

Preston Dickinson: 1891-1930

Preston Dickinson studied at the Art Students' League, and was in Paris from 1910 to 1915. He was at first strongly influenced by the Japanese print, which had been so significant for French painting toward the end of the nineteenth century. Later he was inspired by Cézanne. Dickinson's painting then grew more abstract, in company with that of other important American painters during the decade beginning in 1910.

The influence of the Japanese print appears to have persisted in Dickinson's work, for his paintings continued to have a brittle, two-dimensional aspect, with emphasis on linear design and on ringing decorative color. When he dealt with city and factory subjects, excellent material as they may be for the abstract painter, there was a surface quality of tastefulness that did not get to the heart of the matter.

Dickinson's later paintings of old Quebec are stronger. He was by then an entirely sophisticated and resourceful painter. The subject-matter, however, indicates a special response to the picturesque—a feeling for the aesthetic point of view as something apart from mundane experience. In the long run, Dickinson avoided the challenge of the familiar; growing weary of his surroundings, he first tried Canada, then returned to Europe and died in Spain in 1930.

8. Old Quarter, Quebec, 1927

Max Weber: 1881-

Max Weber was born in Russia, and reached America by the time he was ten. He grew up in Brooklyn. He studied at the Pratt Institute, and later taught painting in the public schools of Lynchburg, Virginia, and at the State Normal School in Duluth, Michigan. He was able to make his way to Paris by 1905, where for four years he was in the middle of the art stream of the time. He came to know the primitive painter Henri Rousseau, and Guillaume Apollinaire, the critic, poet and spokesman for the young moderns. He knew Picasso—they were the same age—and he studied with Matisse. He helped organize Matisse's first class in 1907, made a summer trip to Spain to study Greco, Velasquez and Goya, and to Italy, where he was impressed by the sculptured simplicity of Giotto, Masaccio and Piero della Francesca. Back in Paris, he had an opportunity to see the great Cézanne exhibition of 1907.

By 1909 he was home in America, with the long climb toward recognition ahead. He had a one-man show at the Haas Gallery that same year, and it was there that Arthur B. Davies bought two of his paintings. Stieglitz showed him along with Marin, Maurer, Hartley and Dove in 1910, and gave him a one-man show in the following year. In 1912, he was invited by Roger Fry to show with the Grafton group in London, where Kandinsky was the only other foreigner. That same year—it was the year of the Armory Show—John Cotton Dana gave him an exhibition at the Newark Museum. The Museum of Modern Art included him in "Nineteen Living Americans" in 1929, and gave him an exhibition in 1930. He is being given another retrospective exhibition by the Whitney Museum in 1949.

In these days of abstract revivalism it is important to recall that Weber, like a number of his contemporaries in the Stieglitz group, was painting cubist and abstract paintings around 1910. Weber followed Picasso through Cubism; more than any other American he has caught Picasso's zeal for experimentation and variety of style. He resembles a musician who is interpreter as well as composer, and he has created highly personal variations which are other painters' delight. His special contribution lies in the poignancy, the pathos, the religious mood which pervades his canvases; his passive female nudes with heavy Assyrian faces have an inalienable splendor; and his bearded elderly men, literate and disputatious, are agitated with the brutality of the times.

9. Whither Now?, 1939

9

Lyonel Feininger: 1871-

Lyonel Feininger went to Europe at the age of sixteen—the year was 1887. He stayed for the major part of a lifetime, mostly in Germany: the rise of the Nazis determined his return home in 1937, some fifty years later. His family had migrated to Charleston, South Carolina, after the revolution of 1848 and his father fought for the South in the Civil War. Shortly afterward Carl Feininger moved his family to New York, where Lyonel was born. Carl Feininger became a concert violinist of international renown and there were concert tours in South America and Europe. Young Feininger grew up in New York. He played a violin in concerts from the age of twelve, and when he sailed for Hamburg it was to study music.

But once in Germany, Feininger decided to become a painter and proceeded to study art in Hamburg and Berlin. He worked as an illustrator for periodicals in Berlin and then in Paris, and he managed to keep up his connection with America, making drawings for *Harper's* in the nineties and doing a double-page comic strip for the *Chicago Tribune* in 1906. He came in contact with Cubism on a trip to Paris in 1911, and from then on the manipulations of geometric forms became his obsession. The cubist painting of the inventors of the style—Picasso, Braque and Gris—had cooled by then, for the cubist fervor was intellectual. But Feininger managed to load Cubism with emotion. He kept enough representation to allow the beholder to enter the painting, and he maintained a definite atmosphere. Geometric structures appear to be established by controlled light as arresting as searchlights thrown on the sky or as the shadows of city buildings on night mist. His language is light itself, and in this respect he is a twentieth-century Turner. Being cubist, his paintings are intellectual; being German, they are emotional and tense; and being American they are extremely romantic.

Feininger taught at the Bauhaus, the art and architecture center organized in Germany by Walter Gropius after the First World War. When the Museum of Modern Art included him in its "Nineteen Living Americans" in 1929, the New York critics were hostile—Feininger had been too long outside the family. In 1931, he was given a major retrospective exhibition in the National Gallery in Berlin and two years later he was hung in the "degenerate art" exhibitions of the Nazis. He came to California to teach in Mills College in 1936, and the following year he returned home for good. In 1944 the Museum of Modern Art gave Feininger an exhibition simultaneously with one of Marsden Hartley.

10. Glorious Victory of the Sloop "Maria", 1926

52

Morris Kantor: 1896-

Morris Kantor was born in Russia, like a number of other outstanding American painters. He came to America in 1911, studied at the Independent School of Art and exhibited yearly with the Independent during the twenties. He was in France in 1927 and he appears, like Weber, to have been strongly influenced by Picasso. He has had his ventures both with abstraction and with bold expressive patterns that arrest an emotion. His color is sober but can be resonant when he wishes.

The convention of modern painting that appears to have most meaning for Kantor is the double image, the presentation of more than one point of view, or of more than one aspect, in the same canvas. This can take many forms; it became the stock-in-trade of the Surrealists. As Tchelitchew has used it with disquieting skill, and Dali with startling agility, one sees either one image or the other, and the technique itself becomes the subject-matter, as in the case of a play on words. Kantor does something more obvious, but with more dignity. He simply brings together what is before the eye and what rises in the mind. In *Farewell to Union Square*, the Square and the flowers, images unrelated in scale, compose on canvas and in the artist's thoughts. The painter gives us a balance between an inner and outer life.

In this Kantor is simply developing something that is native to him. His early paintings, which show a room and a scene through a window, are forerunners: an inner sheltered world is set against an outside world in the most natural way. Later, Kantor presents the inside and outside of a house in less logical, more imaginative form. Going a step further, he sometimes sets together figures that are obviously different images of the same person. This is a literary interest, but it is pursued with plastic means by a painter who has great respect for the texture and surface of the canvas.

11. Farewell to Union Square, 1931

11

John Marin: 1870-

John Marin is America's foremost water-colorist; only in advanced age, during the last decade, has he turned seriously to oils. He paints mountain, pine, rock and sea: the Maine coast has been to Marin what it was to Winslow Homer in an earlier day.

Marin has gleaned what he needed from the Modern movement without being of it. An original and solitary temperament, he lived in Paris during a vital epoch— between 1905 and 1911—without being aware of the experiments which went on around him. What he discovered was himself, and he drifted into that discovery late. His early etchings and water colors were in the Whistler and Impressionist tradition, but as he developed, his style grew more stenographic; a few basic indications contented him. Edward Steichen, photographer friend of Stieglitz, saw Marin's paintings and brought them to New York, and Stieglitz exhibited them in 1909. It was only in Stieglitz's gallery, when Marin returned from his vagabondage, that he discovered what was happening in Europe. That, and the impact of New York as he saw it with a fresh eye, broke the doldrum calm in which he had lived, and he began to picture the strident excitement of a new age.

Marin had studied as an architect and he had a sense of form and scale. He was musical and thought of his paintings in terms of musical compositions. He set a fragment of one scene in the midst of another, producing a harmony where there had only been a melody before. Discontented with the monotony of the rectangular frame, he let his compositions frame themselves with bold irregular border lines. Marin's detachment from the frame resembled his detachment from the Modern movement: he is bounded by it yet aloof.

The Museum of Modern Art gave him a major one-man show in 1936. Eleven years later the Institute of Contemporary Art, together with the Phillips Memorial Gallery and the Walker Art Center in Minneapolis, held a second retrospective exhibition of his works. Marin now spends his winters in Cliffside, New Jersey, and the rest of the year paints at his isolated home on the coast of Maine.

12. Deer Isle, Boats, and Pertaining Thereto, 1927

Karl Knaths: 1891-

Karl Knaths is one of the earlier painters, like Feininger and Stuart Davis, who accepted abstract art as a permanent form of expression; he stands in sharp contrast to those painters of his generation who used it as a discipline and then turned back toward representation. Born in Wisconsin, Knaths studied at the Art Institute of Chicago. He saw the Armory Show when it came to Chicago, and it had the same decisive influence on his work that it had on Davis. The formal and expressive canvases of such men as Matisse, Picasso, Braque, Klee and Kandinsky changed Knaths' conception of the very nature of the art of painting. By the time he had assimilated the work of these artists, he had a style of his own.

The proportions of abstraction and realism have varied in Knaths' work. But the underlying representation is rarely lost and is usually explicit. There is a certain native freshness; although the paintings are studio pieces, they are free of the heavier architectural quality of country paintings done in cities; most of them were created in Provincetown, where Knaths has lived since 1919. Boats, fish, and Knaths' ubiquitous rooster recur both as symbols and subject-matter.

Knaths has humor and color and his lightness of touch is an equivalent for atmosphere. He utilizes the spaces of bare canvas, and creates accurately adjusted compositions with minimal means. His long-studied balance between geometry and representation has brought him increasing power and freedom.

13. Maritime, 1931

13

Charles Sheeler: 1883-

Charles Sheeler has lived and worked through the transition from the days of the American realists to those of the moderns influenced by developments in Europe. He underwent the discipline of abstraction, like so many other painters, during the decade of the Armory Show. His concern with architecture smoothed the way for a return to objectivity and he soon adopted a realism of sharp edges and simplified forms.

Sheeler studied applied design at the School of Industrial Art in his native Philadelphia, and was later a pupil of William M. Chase in New York. He traveled twice to Europe with Chase's class, and took a third trip by himself in 1909. By 1912 he had taken up photography for a living, and it was to have far more influence on his art than his years in art school. The days of slashing brushwork were forgotten, and he developed a technique suited to the clarity of his vision.

Sheeler's painting parallels his work with the camera; for him photography offers a single image, painting a composite that, as William Carlos Williams has said, "prevents these media from being competitive." Photography accounts "for the visual world with an exactitude not equalled by any other medium"; in his paintings he employs a style that removes "the method . . . as far as possible from being an obstacle in the .. consideration of the content of the picture."

Sheeler's machine-tool precision creates an image of the machine age. He presents a world without atmosphere in which no people are to be seen; there is only the evidence of their existence. He is unequaled in his semi-abstract reports on sweatless industrial scenes. They appear to be conjured out of blueprints, and correspond closely to a certain American concept of industry—at once highly organized, idealized, and detached from humanity.

Sheeler is also fascinated by the Pennsylvania farm; he concentrates on utensils and tools, recreating the world that antedated the industrial era.

Whether the tools or complex machines in Sheeler's paintings are of the past or a present age, he conveys the impression that they are comprehended, and draws deeply on the American aesthetic response to mechanism. *Upper Deck*, a turning point in Sheeler's work, is the first painting in which he completed his structure before he began to paint.

14. Upper Deck, 1929

14

Marsden Hartley: 1877-1943

One of the few American painters who achieved a synthesis between the American tradition and powerful European influences, Marsden Hartley absorbed both the sense of structure found in French art and the emotionalism of German painting. He shares this distinction with Lyonel Feininger; the two painters, otherwise so dissimilar, are alike in accomplishment.

Hartley was born in Lewiston, Maine, where he spent his childhood. Later his family moved to Cleveland and he enrolled at the Cleveland School of Art. He came on to New York, studying at the Chase School in 1898 and the National School of Design in 1901. Each summer thereafter he returned to his native Maine to paint.

In his first exhibition, put on by Stieglitz in 1909, Hartley's "black landscapes" were seen to be influenced by Albert Pinkham Ryder, the American mystic. There is a lonely and icy splendor in Hartley's paintings, and his skies, like Ryder's, are weighted with glacial clouds, the heaviest objects in view.

Stieglitz and Arthur B. Davies helped Hartley get to Europe in 1912. He tried his hand at Cubism in Paris and, like Feininger, went to Germany, remaining in Berlin and Dresden during the early years of the First World War. From then on he was a wanderer: he lived in Provincetown and Ogunquit, in Bermuda and New Mexico; and again in Berlin; in Vienna, Italy, Paris, and in the south of France. Home again in 1930, he turned once more to New England, to Gloucester and Cape Ann. In the mid-thirties Hartley was painting in Maine and Nova Scotia. He died in 1943 in Ellsworth, Maine.

As an internationalist, Hartley achieved a native American expression. A poet, an articulate man with words, his painting is nevertheless monosyllabic. Simplified color offsets his intense values. He was at once a gregarious man and a lonely seer. Hartley knew how to profit by the paradox that old Europe was developing a crude new way of seeing and feeling that could be applied to a raw new continent.

15. Fox Island, Maine, 1937–38

Stuart Davis: 1894-

Stuart Davis' father was art director of the *Philadelphia Press*; Sloan, Luks, Glackens and Shinn worked for him, and Henri was a friend. The elder Davis shifted to the *Newark Evening News* at about the time the Philadelphia painters moved to New York. Stuart Davis was brought up in the midst of painting and painters and left High School to enter Henri's class in 1910. He thrived on Henri's criticism, and—in the spirit of the Ash-can School—on the equally liberating atmosphere of Hoboken barrooms; Glenn Coleman was his "guide and counsellor" by night. Davis was illustrating for the old *Masses* by 1913; inspired by Aubrey Beardsley, he was using black-and-white in patterns that presaged the bold abstractions of his later work.

On his own admission, the Armory Show was the greatest single influence Davis experienced. Unlike the older painters who took up abstraction for a decade and returned to a more disciplined realism, his shift to abstract painting was progressive and permanent. First came the influence of Gauguin and Van Gogh, for their symbolic use of color; then about 1920 the influence of Leger and a complete change to poster compositions which made use of letters and flat design. Davis strove from that date for a synthesis between representation and abstraction. Recognizable objects are strewn over a more abstract field, and the different degrees of abstraction in the same canvas create tensions that are echoed by his brilliant color values. Yet Davis' paintings are always based on actual scenes, not merely in the details, but in the larger design as well. This naturalistic source lifts his painting above the dry monotony that haunts the abstractionists, and gives it its fresh American tang.

In 1927 Davis set himself a year's discipline in subject-matter by nailing an egg-beater to a table. The resultant "eggbeater series" became famous. The Whitney Museum bought several of his paintings and he was able to spend a year in Paris. The city fascinated him; a stronger tendency toward representation crept into his paintings and his color grew softer. But when he was back in America he turned to harder, larger, and bolder compositions.

In the thirties Davis painted murals, taught at the Art Students' League, worked on the W.P.A. project and plunged into the Artists' Congress activities. By the forties he had returned to easel painting. The Museum of Modern Art gave him a one-man retrospective exhibition in 1945.

16. Red Cart, 1932

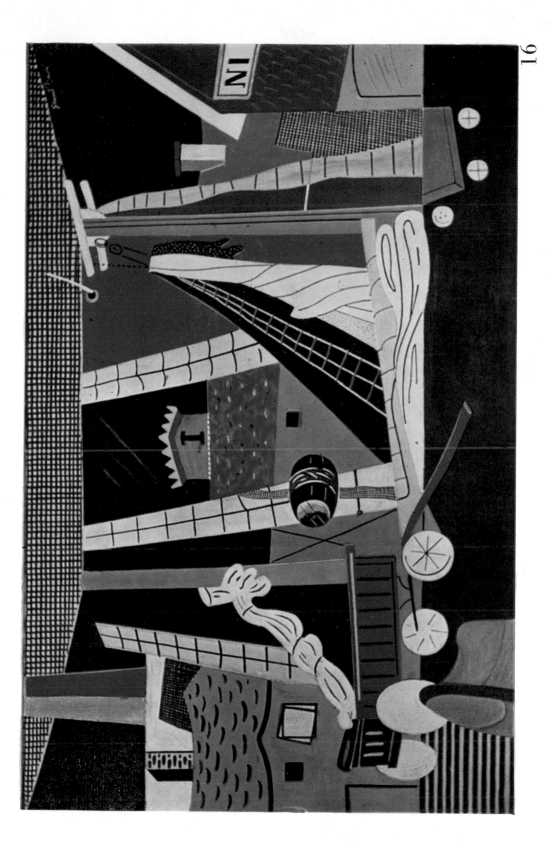

Edward Hopper: 1882-

Edward Hopper was born in the same year as George Bellows. But Hopper got started more slowly; by the time Bellows' life was over Hopper was just beginning to be known. This delay in recognition may have allowed Hopper an easier transition from the days of realism to the days of structure. But the problem was simpler for him, since architecture was his subject. The geometry was already there.

Along with Bellows, Hopper was a pupil of Henri's, and he studied under Kenneth Hayes Miller. He discovered the Impressionists and went to Paris in 1906, earning the money for his trip as an illustrator, an uncongenial labor to which his lack of success as a painter held him for many years. He sold his first canvas out of the Armory Show in 1913. Then he dropped from sight; when he began to command attention again it was through his etchings. The Whitney Studio gave him a show in 1919 and he had another one-man show in 1924. At about that time he sold a water color to the Brooklyn Museum, his second sale in twenty-three years.

Hopper is a fine etcher, and his early plates have a kinship with Sloan's. He is an outstanding water-colorist. His oils, stripped to the essentials, tend toward barrenness, since they are often conceived on too large a scale. His starkness of technique is matched by a starkness of subject. He paints a solitary building, which seems to be the goal of some lonesome quest in his memory; or he paints a city where the search and sense of loneliness persist, where people eat in restaurants or sleep in cheap hotels or sit late in movie-house lobbies for want of a home. His lonely city is New York, and his country, seen in the sharp light of conscience, is the New England coast.

The railroad has been a constant symbol of Hopper's desire to reach a goal, to communicate, to master the scale of the American landscape. In subject-matter his canvases are part of the "American Scene" survey, but they are so steeped in intensity, so imbued with romantic recollection that they become a biography as well as a report.

Hopper has in his best work a monolithic nobility that reflects a personal simplicity, dedication and reticence.

17. Dawn in Pennsylvania, 1942

Charles Burchfield: 1898-

Burchfield is a regional painter. He grew up in Salem, Ohio, and studied at the Cleve-land School of Art. During the twenties he lived in Buffalo, supporting himself as a wallpaper designer. After 1929 he was able to give his full time to painting, and he moved to Gardenville, outside Buffalo, where he still lives.

Burchfield is primarily a water-colorist, and landscapes and townscapes are his subject-matter. He has justly been compared to Sherwood Anderson, the author of *Winesburg, Ohio*. Both men are haunted by a romantic nostalgia, by an ability to see the awesome in the commonplace, the exalted in the drab. Burchfield also has much in common with Edward Hopper, sharing his ability to project human history and personality into houses and buildings. Hopper is less imaginative, gaining power through restraint. Burchfield effervesces into fantasy: the realistic and the fantastic divide his work into two separate categories.

Fantasy came first. From 1916 to 1920 Burchfield produced a series of eerie water colors in which houses grin, and trees, plants and icicles become grotesque manifesta-tions. The imagery fluctuates between the prankish and the sinister, anticipating Walt Disney. Burchfield owes no debt to the European painters of fantasy or to the Surrealists. In the early twenties he passed through a period of discouragement, during which he destroyed his work.

Burchfield's realistic paintings are somber in mood. He is expert in the handling of light to create an emotional atmosphere, whether it is the blank white light of noon that sets off the bleak limitations of a small town, or a winter's twilight that silhouettes houses and just reveals the new moon. In *November Evening* Burchfield has brought together a sweep of plain and the false-fronted main-street buildings which pretend that the town is a city. The buildings. the plain, and the dray in the foreground stand for years of recollection. The painting is not a particular scene: it is a regional novel in itself.

18. November Evening, 1934

Reginald Marsh: 1898-

Reginald Marsh is fascinated by the raw life of New York, the same world which absorbed John Sloan a generation earlier: the loungers on piers, the people who have to raise their voices when the elevated train goes by, the crowds at Coney Island, and above all the burlesque show. Marsh studied under Sloan and later under Kenneth Hayes Miller. But since his parents were artists, he was, like Stuart Davis, brought up in the midst of painting.

At Yale, Marsh drew cartoons for the *Record*, of which he was art editor. Later he worked as a staff artist on *Vanity Fair* and the *Daily News*. He covered vaudeville for the *News*. When he took up painting, his interest in the theatre continued, and he still looked at New York with a reporter's eye.

In 1925 and 1928, Marsh was in Paris, where he spent time copying Rubens and Delacroix in the Louvre; he was influenced by their glowing color, their exuberance, their fluent composing of crowds of figures. Marsh has an ingratiating technique, transparent and brilliant, which suits his subject-matter. He paints the crowd itself rather than individuals; he imparts the general response to light, glare and noise, and conveys a diffuse sensuality.

Yet from time to time Marsh paints a picture in which the figures are more than types, when the loneliness which makes crowds has caught up with them. In *Why not use the "L"?* Marsh rises above himself. He has made a composition out of three people who are strangers, and thus painted the portrait of a city.

19. Why not use the "L", 1930

The Subway is fast—Certainly!
But the Open Air Elevated
gets you there quickly, too
—and with more comfort.

Why not use the "L"?

Thomas Benton: 1899-

No one has a better claim to the legacy of American frontier life: Thomas Benton was the great-nephew of the great and first senator from Missouri, and he grew up on the edge of the Ozarks. Benton's father was a lawyer, and wished his son to follow his profession. But Benton's ambition was for art. He went to the school of the Chicago Art Institute, and insisted on going to Paris.

There for four years he threw himself into the conventional life of the artist, building up his disdain, the while, for the internationalist and expatriate. He returned to New York with an ill-digested modernism, and slugged it out through six years of hard times. The First World War put him in the Navy as a draftsman, and the enforced concern with man's equipment and accomplishments cleared his vision. He saw the whole United States as his model, and when he was out of the service he expanded his scale to become a mural painter.

He returned to Missouri in the mid-twenties and discovered his inheritance. From there he made excursions through the Midwest and the South, feasting on the American scene: the open ranges and the oil derricks, the wheat fields and the cotton lands. A series of murals encompassing this experience made him progressively famous through the nineteen-thirties: at the New School for Social Research, at the Whitney Museum; in the State of Indiana's "Century of Progress" mural, and in the mural for the Missouri State Capitol. These major works have been interspersed with easel paintings; Benton's output has kept pace with his subject-matter.

Benton created a style to intensify his communication; a gnarled distortion touches the figures with caricature, and continues through the whole composition, tightening it like a coiled spring. But his insistence on burliness often strikes a self-conscious note, and blocks the very sense of physical contact for which he sacrifices so much. He tends to substitute violence for emotion.

In the early Western paintings, such as *Cattle Loading, West Texas*, there was something which fitted the subject and will be hard to regain, the brash delight of adventure and discovery.

20. Cattle Loading, West Texas, 1930

72

Grant Wood: 1892-1942

Grant Wood was born in Anamosa, Iowa, and his family soon moved to Cedar Rapids. A Quaker upbringing and extreme poverty made his boyhood bleak and hard; he supported his mother and sister after his father's death when Grant was only ten.

The First World War gave Wood a wider horizon. When he returned to Cedar Rapids he obtained a position teaching art, and somehow he managed to get to Italy and France in the summers. After seven years he received a commission for a stained-glass window from the American Legion, and he went to Munich for two years to learn how to make it. This venture had important results. Local patriotism took it ill that the window was made in Germany; the D.A.R. fought beside the Legion and the window was never erected. But Wood came out of the battle with his satirical painting, *Daughters of Revolution*.

During his two years in Germany, Wood fell under the spell of the German primitives and the Flemish painters. In these, skill and sincerity were concentrated on a precise factual rendering until even the trivial became intense; and the uncompromising and shadowless faces in the old paintings reminded Wood of his countrymen at home. Such an art could convey the stark protestant integrity of the world he had known. On his return, Wood adopted this style, precise, archaic, yet in his hands sincere, and began to paint the world about him. His *American Gothic* made him famous. The painting was as fine as its title, which incidentally confessed the source of his change in style.

From then on Wood produced few paintings, seeking subjects which would allow him to concentrate much experience into each. In this he resembled Curry; but he was more uneven than Curry. If he had greater technical resources, there were times when they failed him. Whenever the emotion ran thin, his paintings were contrived and degenerated into the quaint.

Since Wood's painting was often loaded with satire, he had his troubles with local pride; but eventually the region came to his support, the University of Iowa appointing him artist-in-residence.

21. American Gothic, 1930

21

John Steuart Curry: 1897-1946

Real ability and an inherent lack of sophistication marked Curry with a certain innocence, particularly as compared with Benton and Wood, the two westerners with whom he was closely associated. In style, in concentration on a dramatic subject, he was coeval with Sloan or the early Bellows, a fact that is not at once apparent, since Benton and Wood tended to sweep him along into a later tense. Curry was completely dependent on his subject, and he gave himself over to it with naïve devotion. As a result, his few paintings are monuments to the life in Kansas which he recalled.

His groups of figures are compact, and often close to sculpture—monumental in a literal sense, so that there is more composition in the relations of the figures than on the surface of the canvas. There are few outside influences to blunt the thrust of his sincerity; he has the primitive characteristic of being at once at his best. His later paintings, in which the composition is consciously forced, are below his top level.

Curry was born on a farm in Dunavant, Kansas, and left high school for a job as a section hand on the railroad. Intent on painting, he supported himself for two years while attending the Chicago Art Institute, and he spent the next five years struggling as an illustrator for "Western" magazines. He then borrowed a thousand dollars and went to Paris for a year—but there is hardly a trace of that experience in his work. On his return, he challenged himself to paint one good painting or quit, and he produced *Baptism in Kansas*. The painting was bought by Mrs. Whitney, who then subsidized Curry for two years. At the end of that time—it was 1930—Curry hit another high point in *Tornado over Kansas*.

He taught at Cooper Union for a while, and at the Art Students' League. Again he went through a cycle of discouragement, soul-searching, and success, at the end producing *Line Storm* from his early memories. He painted murals for the Departments of Justice and of the Interior in Washington, and in the Kansas State capitol at Topeka, and he was selected by the College of Agriculture of the University of Wisconsin as artist-in-residence.

22. Baptism in Kansas, 1925

22

Ben Shahn: 1898-

Ben Shahn, like Weber, was born in Russia, came to this country as a child of eight, and grew up in Brooklyn. He worked as a lithographer's apprentice while attending night school, and relied on lithography for support until he was in his thirties. Possibly for this reason, drawing is the backbone of his art. But Shahn also needs line to communicate, for his painting is loaded with social convictions and is meant to be read. He turns without difficulty from easel painting to murals or to posters—to whichever medium best allows him to reach his audience.

He was abroad in the twenties, and took what he could from the school of Paris. In fact, he believed that he had taken too much, and in a moment of self-questioning he threw away what was alien to his new-found purpose. He then painted his famous Sacco and Vanzetti series. Diego Rivera saw these paintings and employed him as his assistant. Shahn's next series covered the Mooney case.

During the thirties Shahn was enrolled in the Public Works Art Project. He took up photography which has since provided him with his preliminary material; and he saw much of America while working as artist and photographer for the Farm Security Administration.

His murals for Rikers Island prison were disapproved and never executed. His earliest finished mural is in the community center of Jersey Homesteads at Roosevelt, New Jersey, where he still lives. He completed murals for the Bronx Post Office in New York in 1939 and, fittingly, for the Social Security Building in Washington in 1942.

It is Shahn's strength that his intense human sympathies escape doctrinaire generalizations; they are based on the plight of the individual. The scene he creates is all the more moving in that very often his actors are contented. He has remarkable insight into the lives of children, especially as they play in a world of make-believe that parallels our own. Shahn's people loaf when they can, and entertain themselves with musical instruments. His politicians are not monsters, they are only trivial people, superfluous in a world they can sometimes reduce to rubble. In *Fourth of July Orator*, the minute scale of the would-be demagogues and the wide space of untrodden grass around them testify to American political health and to Shahn's humor in the midst of his sincerity.

23. Fourth of July Orator, 1943

William Gropper: 1897-

There is justification in calling Gropper the American Daumier; he is a cartoonist of power who turned to painting relatively late. Growing up with a generation in which class-consciousness was an expression of human sympathy, the bulk of his early work was mordant cartoons published in the *Rebel Worker* and in the *New Masses*. He was born on New York's East Side and at fourteen he was working for a dollar a day in a sweat shop. It was a twelve-hour day in a six-day week. He has remained loyal to this world, and has not felt that it was a privilege to succeed and forget it.

Gropper had been painting for years before he brought his canvases forward in 1936. Subsequently he painted a mural in the Freeport, Long Island, Post Office on the W.P.A., and another mural for the Department of the Interior. His shift to paint marked no shift in subject-matter: his paintings were still cartoons. He was already a master of simplification and of essential gesture, and caught the eye with action. It is his weakness and strength that what one sees is not an individual but a single characteristic act—and always an act with moral implications.

Gropper has also been an illustrator of myth, American or universal: Paul Bunyan, Paul Revere, the Headless Horseman, Diogenes. When indignation is absent, Gropper appears as a romantic—and as something less than his characteristic self. Too strident for fantasy, he sometimes sinks to the grotesque.

In the early days of the war Gropper attacked isolationism, particularly as it talked and balked in the Senate. *Isolationist* is one of a series, and, like the senator depicted, speaks for itself. This is using paint with integrity, intensity, and power.

24. Isolationist

Mitchell Siporin: 1910-

Born in New York, Mitchell Siporin grew up in Chicago and studied at the school of the Chicago Art Institute. His painting concerns itself with injustice and with man's plight. In company with Levine and Shahn he draws on a strong social consciousness for subject-matter and for the drive behind his work. He looks to the prophetic and majestic spirits for inspiration: to Lincoln, Whitman, Dostoievsky, Orozco —to Vachel Lindsay as spokesman for his region of the country. Yet Siporin does not escape one of the limitations of the time. His social thinking and his venerations run to type, and his painting tends to run to type, even in the figures and faces. In this he differs from Shahn and Levine, who base the drama on individuality. In Siporin, the absence of the individual makes the allegory heavy; but with this reservation, he is a painter of power.

Siporin belongs to the generation that came to maturity during the depression. He has been truck driver and scene painter. He painted murals for the W.P.A., was one of three painters commissioned by the Public Building Administration to paint frescoes for the Post Office at Decatur, Illinois, and, with one of his collaborators, won a competition for seventeen frescoes for the Post Office in St. Louis. His broad concepts lend themselves to the architectural scale, and his painting is legible to all.

His easel paintings communicate as freely as his murals: men by a railroad track stand for refugees, and their shack shelters a madonna and child. A man hedged by a barbed-wire entanglement is surrounded by figures that symbolize his hopes: it is the *Dream of the Good Life*.

25. Dream of the Good Life, 1941

Abraham Rattner: 1893-

When he had his first sight of Paris, Rattner was a G.I. in the First World War. He had already studied at the Pennsylvania Academy of Fine Arts, and soon after his return to America the Academy granted him a traveling scholarship that allowed him to go back to France. The scholarship ran out, but Rattner managed to stay on. The post-war generation came home; but Rattner continued to paint in Paris until the German invasion.

If Rattner was able to transplant himself for so long without losing his identity, it was because of a native intensity of character. He brought with him and maintained a fervor of integrity that was proof against the inviting diffuseness with which Paris beguiles the foreigner once the expansive years of discovery are past. For Rattner, Paris was a "temple of art and the spirit." It gave him "the feeling of living the way the Bible reads." But that phrase might also describe the beholder's feelings in the presence of Rattner's painting, and is certainly an odd description for the liberalizing influence of the French capital.

Rattner's painting is sternly moral; there is much in it of Picasso, of the Byzantine influence, and of Rouault. Black lines bound vivid slabs of color and lock the figures in hieratic attitudes. On the one hand there are burning spiritual themes; on the other Rattner insists on the priority over subject of formal and painterly considerations. Instead of dividing the interest, this double allegiance to abstraction and an austere humanism heightens the impact of his art.

Many of Rattner's paintings deal with the brotherhood or the ferocity of men. His compositions confront the beholder with a solid phalanx of humanity; the device of a series of heads in which the left eye of one is the right eye of the next (in itself a Byzantine conception) allows Rattner to show us the impersonal brutality of soldiers at the crucifixion. In a different and rarer mood, it allows the artist to organize the confused impression of a city crowd in *April Showers*. The umbrellas create a fragile city architecture of their own, which is not without its humor. Except for the flowers, the whole canvas is green: a color called to mind by the spring rain.

26. April Showers, 1939

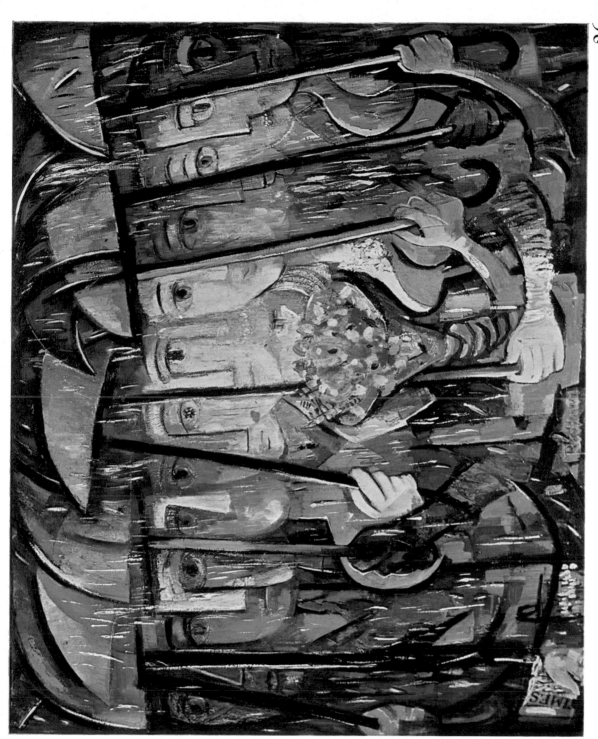

George Grosz: 1893-

French painting, which has had such an influence on the art of the rest of the world, is geographically self-centered; it is rare that a French painter becomes an American. By contrast, important German painters have come to America and entered American life. George Grosz and Karl Zerbe came well before the last war; and Feininger, who spent most of his life as a painter in Germany, has returned. One would have liked to include Max Beckmann in this company, but his arrival is so recent that he can hardly be mentioned in the record of American accomplishment.

George Grosz had a style and an international reputation before he reached America. He was essentially a political cartoonist, dedicated to an onslaught on the spirit of oppression and intolerance as he saw it rising in Germany from the ashes of the First World War. But this attack was not in terms of the dramatic, simplified political cartoon as we know it, for instance, in Gropper. Grosz was more subtle and devastating. His drawing often had a child-like simplicity; the more intense his feeling, the more naïvely diagrammatic his drawing appeared. He was able to unleash the helpless hatred of the child for adult injustice, and his child's ferocity was related to the child's fantasy in the drawing of his great Swiss contemporary, Paul Klee. Grosz was an artist of the first rank in his field.

When Grosz came to America a change came over his work. His polemical frenzy died down; he shifted to oils, and to a more serene vision. And this easing of tension dampened the fire in his work, weakening his mordant line.

He kept to the new style when he returned to the political arena to battle once again for moral and spiritual causes; now the vortex and spiral in his composition and brushwork recall Van Gogh and convey a similar agitation of spirit. In *No Let Up* he has achieved in natural terms an allegory in which one can believe: it is a painting of a child in a storm. Where Grosz once conveyed intense feeling through a child's vision, he now shows us a desperate child itself as a symbol of the world's ordeal. The storm which drives it is quite impersonal and inhuman; a single figure in a single canvas carries the artist's whole theme, without any of the symbolic trappings of war.

27. No Let Up, 1940

Jack Levine: 1915-

Jack Levine was the youngest of a family of eight in the slums of Boston's South End. Attending classes at the Boston Museum of Fine Arts he came to the notice of Denman Ross of the Fogg Museum at Harvard and underwent an apprenticeship to a highly systematized scheme of teaching. Levine, however, soon took his career in his own hands; repudiation of any system was essential to his integrity and independence. He had grown up into the depression; working on the W.P.A. he developed a style that rested on a moral rather than an aesthetic base.

The heavy and glittering paint that Levine drags over the canvas, the dark and powerful outlines, come from Rouault; the fluttering shimmer of light over red flesh from Soutine; and from both the anatomical distortion of the gigantically enlarged head. This mannerism of the large head sharpens the satire of the painting, suggesting infantile proportions, as though the characters depicted were child conspirators or the victims of child labor. Levine has learned the language of sincerity and he has the ability to create monumental works of art that have a life and personality of their own. *String Quartette* is such a composition. Characteristically a group of figures is spread in an arc over the canvas, but figures securely tied together by their employment, or self-interest, so that they create a small society complete in itself.

Levine's social awareness is clear and intense. What is valuable to him is to show, not that a man has more than his share of labor, but that he has little—too little—freedom. His instinct as an artist tells him that man is only important when he is free, and Levine is intent on this freedom dearly bought rather than the sordid image of oppression. He has turned to satire of late, and his technique has grown lighter and more subtle; if his painting has gained technically, it has lost in effect, since satire often scales down the importance of the work of art along with the subject.

28. String Quartette, 1934–37

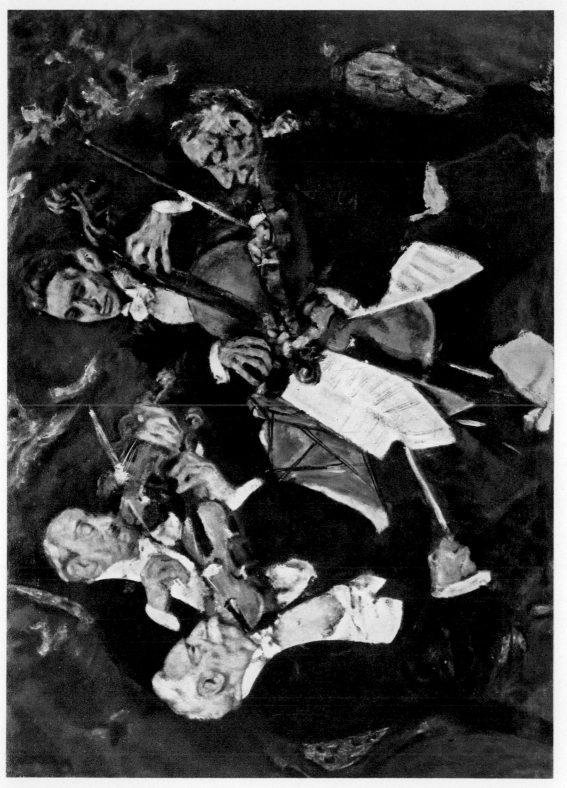

Joseph Hirsch: 1910-

Simplification for the sake of composition, playing with values to force the form, and an occasional excursion into the grotesque are all the freedoms that Joseph Hirsch allows himself. He is a realist; he bathes the scene in atmosphere, continuing the line of the early liberal reporters. Hirsch studied with George Luks in the last year of Luks' life; but where the early reporters favored humanity, the artists of the depression years were not dependent on incident to prompt their indignation or sympathy. To let Hirsch convey his own mood: "The weather has changed, and for all our nostalgia, the fruits of today are not odalisques nor pears and mandolins on a rumpled tablecloth. Ours is an era of accelerated transition; this is the season for weapons."

Such a mood opens the door to propaganda in art, but in his approach Hirsch gains more than he loses. The feeling is strong without being doctrinaire, and never maudlin—except for one war poster. The bite of social conscience often saves him from the picturesque, and he always comes back to the individual, which saves him from generalizations. He is one of the contemporary painters who paints a good portrait. In *Old Man*, where all his best characteristics are present, Hirsch gives us an individual portrait together with a human situation commanding sympathy, and just enough distortion to sharpen the mood.

Hirsch worked on the W.P.A. project, painting murals for the Benjamin Franklin High School in his home town of Philadelphia, and he later had his first exhibition in that city. He was shown by the Amalgamated Meatcutters' Union in New York in 1941 and in the following year was one of the group of eighteen painters presented by the Museum of Modern Art.

29. Portrait of an Old Man, 1939

29

Aaron Bohrod: 1907-

In *Landscape in Chicago*, Bohrod at once paints a literal fragment of the American scene and underscores an aspect of a whole society. He is a painter of social protest, but he does not use the editorial method or symbolize man's plight; instead he contents himself with reporting, with letting facts and human beings speak for themselves. He paints the monotonous drab life of the depressed areas of cities, above all of his native Chicago, and he portrays this existence in terms of its environment.

Bohrod's father came to America from Russia, and opened a grocery store in Chicago. After supporting himself while attending the school of the Art Institute, young Bohrod came to New York to study with John Sloan at the Art Students' League, and was twice granted a Guggenheim Fellowship.

Being a painter of city scenes and a pupil of Sloan's, Bohrod's work shows resemblances to that of the Ash-can School, but the mood is new. In Bohrod, the exuberance of the early radicals has given place not only to a stronger social concern, but to a more somber tone, which the paint itself, with its muted gray grounds, reflects.

Bohrod was one of the most successful of the painters who covered the war. He escaped the official attitude and he did not attempt to out-clamor the subject; his paintings of campaigns in the Pacific are moving in their understatement. His canvases are small, and the men in them are on a small scale: he reports bluntly on the triviality of death in a mechanized world.

30. Landscape near Chicago, 1934

Milton Avery: 1893-

Milton Avery was born in New York state and moved to Hartford, Connecticut, in 1905. He began to paint when he was twenty and studied for a while at the Connecticut League of Art Students. With a minimum of instruction Avery developed a highly personal style; his early paintings were narrow and somber panels which suggest the work of Soutine and the Picasso of the Blue Period. A little later he was making use of clear color in a two-dimensional pattern, and he began to be told that he then resembled Matisse and the radical painters who assaulted Paris with color in the first decade of the century. But Avery's concern was simply with paint and pattern; he would go out into the Connecticut countryside to work after an eight-hour night shift in a factory; the only signs of further horizons in his work came from two trips, one to the Gaspé Peninsula and another to California.

Avery married in 1926 and moved to New York. Two years later he had his first one-man show. But his paintings were out of place in the scheme of things: he was an American who was painting with the interests, and the results, of a French colorist at a moment when the recorders of the American scene were coming to the fore. It was the decade of the depression, and Avery's absorption in pure painting was against the trend. Perhaps he did not recognize the depression; his work had been quite misunderstood in his New England environment, and he had always had a difficult time. The result has been recognition for his work rather than popularity.

The Musicians conveys admirably the importance of color to Avery. In the French tradition, such a use of color had sifted down from the Japanese print through Van Gogh, Gauguin and the *Fauves*. But there is something homespun about Avery's painting that acquits it of imitation. His painting also has a natural humor, and a surprisingly high human content for so abstract an art. Yet, like Stuart Davis, he has continued to build an abstract design out of realistic elements, and the colors with which he illuminates New England are as brilliant as autumn leaves.

31. Music Maker, 1946

31

Hyman Bloom: 1913-

Hyman Bloom was born in Latvia. At the age of seven he came to America, to Boston, where he still lives. Like Jack Levine, Bloom studied for a while with Denman Ross of the Fogg Museum at Harvard. Also like Levine he was to veer off into a personal expression, a manner which resembles recent German painting with its contortions and stresses. The color in Bloom's work, however, is more eastern. He has a taste for dazzle and glitter; his synagogue paintings, and his *Chandelier* and *Christmas Tree* flicker with the hues of flame.

In his more recent work Bloom has looked at existence not as a sociologist, but from the view which opens to the medical student; he confronts himself with man's physical boundaries, with factual images of illness and dissolution. He has painted a modern Dance of Death. There are also more abstract canvases, such as *Buried Treasure*, in which he yields to his sense of pure design. His freedom of range, from the realistic through the expressive to formal design, is characteristic of the younger men.

Bloom was shown by the Museum of Modern Art in the *Americans 1942* exhibition, and has since had several one-man shows in Boston and New York.

32. Buried Treasure, 1948

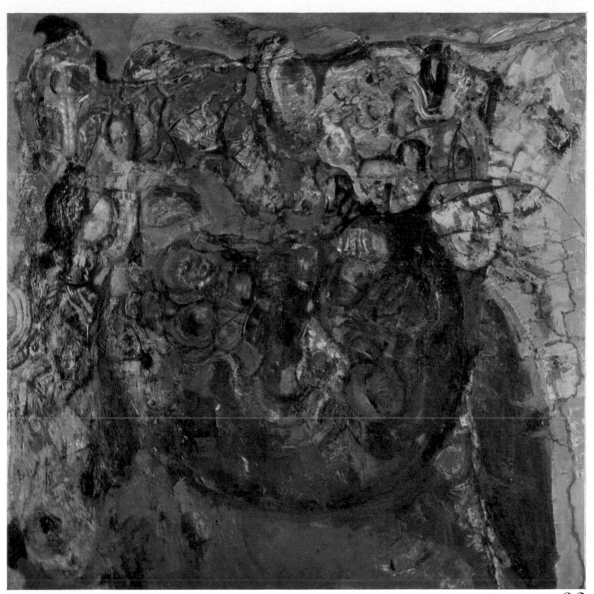

32

Peter Blume: 1906-

Peter Blume is one more of the important American painters who were born in Russia and grew up in Brooklyn. He came to this country when he was twelve. That he worked for engravers and lithographers appears more significant than any schooling which he received. His painting is infinitely precise and specific, and his pencil drawing has a steel-engraving perfection. Yet he is able to organize and control his minutae and paint a large canvas, largely conceived.

Blume mixes styles in a way now characteristic of the painters younger than himself. The transfixed brilliance of his painting and his flair for bringing together objects never associated in real life relate him to the Surrealists. But he does not delve into subconscious associations for shock effect. His painting *South of Scranton* reports on a trip he took in the United States, and the lone mast of the cruiser recalls a German ship he saw in the port of Charleston. The juxtapositions are drawn out of conscious memory and the jumping figures illustrate three positions in a single cross-country leap. The painting presents no more problem than notations in a diary.

Blume's technique is characteristic of painters who work with scientific detachment; one is reminded of Sheeler. But Blume always makes reference to humanity. Figures are always present, and the objects represented are chosen for their significance in experience—often a moral significance. Blume belongs (if we must classify him) among the painters who have dedicated their art to social comment.

South of Scranton won first prize at the Carnegie International Exhibition in 1934. Blume was helped through the thirties by two Guggenheim Fellowships, and he went to Italy, as his *Eternal City* of 1937 records. This ambitious painting is more meticulous and less imposing than *South of Scranton*, undertaking as it does a propaganda theme that calls for poster treatment. But Blume has an instinct for the rare, long-labored, and important work which has won him a high place among American painters.

33. South of Scranton, 1931

Rico Lebrun: 1900-

Rico Lebrun was born in Naples. He began painting early, has persisted through many transplantings and is only now gaining wide recognition. He attended night school at the Naples Academy of Arts, worked in a bank, fought in the Italian Army in the First World War, and later worked in a stained-glass factory in Naples. He came to America in 1924 to establish a branch factory in Springfield, Illinois. The next year he moved to New York.

During the difficult thirties, Lebrun was twice granted a Guggenheim Fellowship. He was commissioned by the Section of Fine Arts of the Public Buildings Administration to paint frescoes for the New York City Post Office Annex. He has taught at the Art Students' League and was one of a group of eighteen Americans exhibited by the Museum of Modern Art in 1942.

Since Lebrun did not grow up in America, he is outside the pattern of American painters assimilating a European tradition. At the same time, he came to this country too early to bring a fixed manner with him. He has been quite willing to move from style to style. There are Rouault and Picasso resemblances, unabashedly close. His surrealist *Migration to Nowhere*, a wild flight of tattered creatures on crutches driven over a plain, is the essence of autobiography. *Vertical Composition,* which won first prize at the Chicago Art Institute's exhibition of Abstract and Surrealist Art in 1946, is a fine design achieved with recognizable means. The upturned axle and wheels tell of wasted effort and wrecked machinery, just as Piranesi's imposing sixteenth-century etchings told of noble architecture that was only man's prison.

Lebrun appears unwilling to restrict or limit his art—he has had too wide an experience. There is a basic realism in his work which is often modified, but never lost.

34. Vertical Composition, 1945

34

Loren MacIver : 1909-

Loren MacIver shows that pliability and freedom which one would expect in the latter phases of a cycle in art. She places emphasis by turns on a simplified realism and on geometric abstraction. In *Sidewalk* she has created a design in which a geometric grid overlays fluid accidental forms. The means are obvious; the artist's eye was caught by chalkmarks on a broken pavement. The result is subtle: in effect the artist brings two styles together and uses the styles themselves as elements of composition.

Miss MacIver singles out objects and broods upon them, drawing out of them the overtones of association. The latent feelings which the object stirs are what she values. "My wish is to make something permanent out of the transitory by means at once dramatic and colloquial. Certain moments have the gift of revealing the past and foretelling the future. It is these moments that I hope to catch."

Loren MacIver was born in New York and studied for about a year at the Art Students' League at the age of ten. From 1936 to 1939 she worked on the W.P.A. project. During these years, she spent the summers on Cape Cod, and she has spent winters in Key West. She had her first one-man show in 1939 and was one of the Museum of Modern Art's group of fourteen American painters exhibited in 1946.

35. The Sidewalk, 1940

35

I. Rice Pereira: 1907-

The boundaries of a technique are conventions which most artists accept: a new result is produced with familiar means. But what if the artist refuses to be bound by any particular means, such as the technique of oil on canvas? Whether the work is painting, sculpture or architecture then no longer matters; that it establishes relationships is enough. Contrasts of any sort allow composition—light against dark, color against color, coarse texture against fine, line against shape, transparent against opaque.

I. Rice Pereira exploits these contrasts with other means besides paint. This throws open an enormous field, for the limits are set only by the artist's interests. Miss Pereira happens to be concerned with rectangular compositions in which one plane hovers over another. Often this is carried out in actuality, rather than in the illusion of paint: a pane of glass, with an abstract pattern painted upon it, is set above an opaque ground which carries a different pattern, and these patterns are contrapuntal to each other. This use of transparency evokes limitless relationships, leading where the eye cannot follow.

The artist is realistically concerned with materials and their properties, with parchment, resin, varnish and lacquer; with mica, marble dust, and goldleaf. For her the special qualities of her materials are significant for the quality of the work of art. Her art is primarily one of arrangement, not of illusion; illusion is only an additional resource.

In *Green Depth*, however, the artist contents herself with paint, and proves that she can create the three-dimensional sense which she requires.

36. Green Depth, 1944

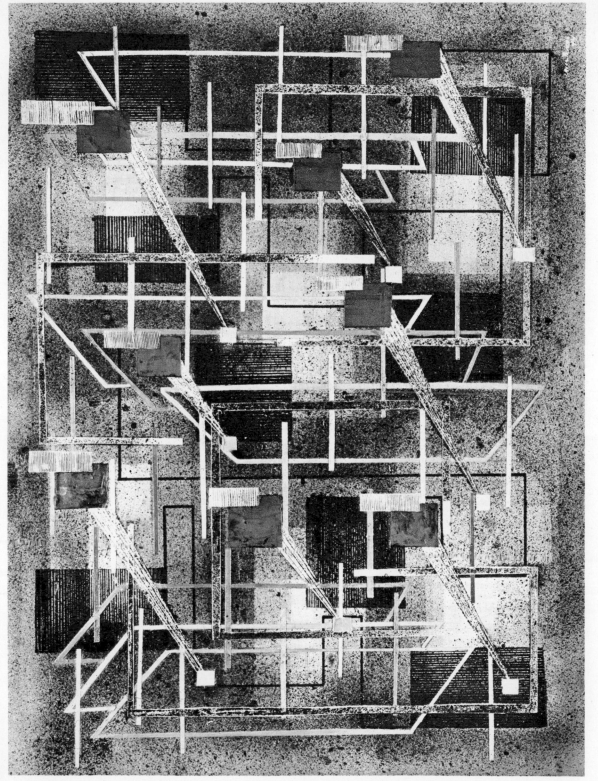

Adolph Gottlieb: 1903-

The later abstract painters have in general allowed themselves to move freely from geometric patterns to those more fluid amorphous images that approach Surrealism. As the artist's work has become less suppressed, the trend has been from architectural forms toward the organic. Many painters have combined both elements in the same canvas, and Adolph Gottlieb is a case in point. In his series of "pictographs" he divides the canvas into compartments with an architectural grid and fills the spaces with images resembling hieroglyphics. These vaguely recognizable symbols arrest and challenge the beholder. Like undeciphered inscriptions, they imply a communication that is not to be lifted into conscious language. For this very reason they stir the emotions, harping on things that hover just out of reach of memory. The somber color tends to a single dominant tone, and helps create a subdued, unbroken mood.

If the resulting art is somewhat monotonous and limited in range, it is the more original for staying within its own territory. Gottlieb studied abroad from 1920 to 1922, and his painting shows the School of Paris interest in the primitive; the "pictographs" remind one of pre-Columbian art, with its absorption in sacrifice and death.

37. Pictograph, 1942

37

Morris Graves: 1910-

Morris Graves is a West Coast painter. Born in Fox Valley, Oregon, he has lived most of his life in the state of Washington. He made a trip to Japan in 1930, and his mystical art admits a strong Oriental influence in the flat ground and in linear design.

Graves is indebted to Mark Toby, Seattle artist of an older generation, whose narrow and sensitive art made use of "white writing." Toby covered a dark surface with scratched or scribbled white lines, creating by this means an impression of brilliance and infinity. Graves added symbols to this white writing, in particular symbolic birds which come to nest in the linear maze. The result is a poetic art with an excitement quite its own. Time and again the bird symbol recurs; it broods, blind, with vast shuttered eyes, sings in the moonlight, or lurks in a mysterious nest or web; or seems to be swept along in a sea of barely visible lines of force as in the *Journey*. The bird apparently signifies some transformation, or migration of spirit.

Such an art is limited unless it has many symbols to offer. And there is this further restriction, that some symbols which are significant to the artist may have little meaning to others. Graves' birds are superbly evocative; then there is the moon, and moonlight which comes tangling down in a dazzling maze of white writing. Furniture, and more recently, Oriental objects of art in process of transformation, seem far less successful. It is only a step from intuitive creation to conscious ingenuity which simulates the miracle.

Although Graves has perhaps chosen a tenuous art, his successes are real. Reaching out as he has to the Orient for inspiration, he has moved outside the Western tradition. He has not only created a personal expression but he has opened up a new sphere.

38. Journey, 1944

Bernard Karfiol: 1886-

America's foremost painter of nudes was considered too young for the life class when he enrolled at the National Academy of Design at the age of fourteen. The year was 1900. A year before he had been warned away from the Pratt Institute—his mother had been told that it was not a kindergarten—and he settled for Cooper Union. A year later he had persuaded his family to send him to Paris.

Young Karfiol was immediately at home in Paris; with the assurance of a man twice his age he sought out the people and the ideas essential to him. He knew Epstein and Fry, Segonzac and Pascin. He knew Leo and Gertrude Stein, who introduced him to Picasso and Matisse and—like Max Weber—he knew Henri Rousseau. If he served his time at Julian's Academy under Bouguereau and Jean Paul Laurens, and went to the Salon, he also discovered the work of Cézanne and Renoir, of Lautrec, Gauguin, Van Gogh and Seurat. He had experienced a half-century of Europe in five years. By 1906 he had returned to America with a wife and two children; he was just twenty years old.

Mrs. Whitney assisted Karfiol, giving him a studio and arranging for him to teach a group of her friends. During this period he moved to Ridgefield, New Jersey, where he still lives. In 1912, Hamilton Field discovered Karfiol's work and bought the first painting the artist had sold in eight years. Field gave Karfiol a small exhibition, along with Marin, in his house on Brooklyn Heights. He bought all the Karfiols in the show and invited the painter to Ogunquit; Karfiol still spends his summers there.

Karfiol's early figures were young and cool in a silvery light, with the wan grace of the early Picasso. Now his nudes are full-bodied and glowing; they look on with a dark, patient glance out of oval faces.

Karfiol's reputation has grown with a quiet inevitability, although he lacks the angle or facet which reflects publicity, and there is nothing strident about his work.

39. Boy, ca. 1925

Henry E. Mattson: 1887-

At once a romantic and a mystic, Mattson recalls the great Albert Pinkham Ryder. For both, the ocean by the light of the moon is a recurrent theme. To be precise, the light in Mattson's painting is neither of the moon (there is too much color) nor of the sun (there is too much mystery) but a mystical effulgence. The painting appears to loom on a dark ground; objects do not appear because they are in sight, but are evoked as they are needed. There is a misty, feathery quality in the paint itself. Mattson is willing to let the surface dissolve. The painter's choice of the vague and atmospheric road to mysticism is a nineteenth-century approach; in this century the mystical has excessive clarity.

Such a detachment from the source of observation tends toward generalization and monotony in an artist's work. Mattson, however, escapes the commonplace by evading the literal. The few objects in his paintings, cloud, sea and rock, are sufficiently amorphous to adapt themselves to his symbolic requirements. The repetition is somehow not wearisome. Since the mood is religious, nearing a pantheism hinted at in the title *Wings of the Morning*, his paintings resemble recurrent rituals. In *Wings of the Morning* three eternal things, the wind, the sea, and the new day, seem to move together into the canvas from the East.

Mattson was born in Sweden; he was nineteen when he came to America. He studied for a while at the Worcester Art Museum and joined the art colony at Woodstock, New York, in 1946. He has lived there ever since and it is there that his imaginary seascapes have been painted.

40. Wings of the Morning, 1937

Franklin C. Watkins: 1894-

A highly romantic and sophisticated painter, Franklin Watkins has built on a broad education in art. There is much of Greco and the Mannerists in his work: the elongated figures, the flickering and agitating forms, the sensitive subdued color. He makes use of atmospheric tonalities, but the atmosphere he creates is also a spiritual one; he is successful in symbolic paintings, like the *Recording Angel*, which seems an achievement removed from our day.

Watkins studied at the Pennsylvania Academy of Fine Arts, and teaches there at the present time. He has had his share of recognition, winning the First Prize at the Carnegie International Exhibition in 1931. But he is a painter's painter, at once outside the trend of painting immediately influenced by Europe and remote from the reporters on the American scene. He is closest to the exaggerations of Expressionism; but his concave forms, lacking in bulk, are quite personal, and his fragile color betrays an ascetic reserved temper. He has done some of the finest portraits painted in America, with a sensibility completely attuned to the sitter.

The *Fire Eater* is somewhat exceptional in its realistic subject-matter. The painter, however, has found an opportunity in the scene for the agitated forms which he favors.

41. Fire Eater, 1933–34

41

Yasuo Kuniyoshi: 1893-

Yasuo Kuniyoshi was born in Japan and came to America as a boy of thirteen with neither money behind him nor friends ahead of him, guided by an optimistic instinct for a career in the western world. He landed in Vancouver, and was soon in Los Angeles, where a turn for drawing led him from the public schools to the Los Angeles School of Art and Design. He worked at a score of jobs, in hotels in winter, and picking fruit in summer. An Asiatic, and an alien as he still by law must be, he belonged to a world whose poverty is not disturbing to Americans at large. Kuniyoshi did not start as a poor artist but as a poor Japanese, and he has met with facility cir-cumstances which would at least have immobilized others.

He came to New York to study in 1910, and moved from one school to another, eventually working for four years under Kenneth Hayes Miller. He was encouraged by the collector Hamilton Field who gave him a studio for two summers at Ogunquit, Maine, and tided him over in New York. For five years he supported himself by photographing paintings, and painted in the summers at Ogunquit. He began to exhibit yearly, and the Museum of Modern Art included him in its "Nineteen Living Americans" show in 1929. He has taught at the Art Students' League and at the New School for Social Research. He was the first living painter to be given a retro-spective show at the Whitney Museum (in 1948) and he has been the president of Artist's Equity since its foundation in 1947.

Kuniyoshi's compositions have the climbing perspective of Oriental art. He is a master of the still-life in which random objects come together in a free association of their own. His paintings of women offer suavity and sensuality. He is a cool romantic who combines the beauty of women and of objects and of paint. The artist's vivacity is in uncanny contrast with the gold and gray detachment, the bleak worldliness of his model. He re-creates the excited yet jaded mood of Western city life.

42. Bouquet and Stove, 1929

42

Pavel Tchelitchew: 1898-

Tchelitchew began as a designer for the stage. Being Russian the theatre and the ballet have always seemed important media to him. He was first influenced by Constructivism, a Russian outgrowth of Cubism. This was in the days when he was working for the theatre in Berlin after the First World War. With this experience in abstract design behind him, he appeared in Paris in 1925 and began to paint. At this time his discovery of the Picasso of the Rose Period liberated his native nostalgia and romantic mood. Like Picasso he became absorbed by the circus and painted a series of acrobats and clowns.

Tchelitchew was the outstanding figure among the Neo-Romantics who emerged as a group in Paris in 1926. He painted in the subdued palette of the Neo-Romantics, which was in harmony with their elegiac temper. But Tchelitchew was too inventive to linger in a single style. He became absorbed in effects of exaggerated perspective, combining in the same canvas different points of view and therefore different moments in time. He played variations on the double-image theme, projecting figures into landscape so that one image is concealed in the other, and recognition fluctuates between them. Veins of vegetation are made to serve for the webbing of blood vessels and nerves in the body, an interplay of imagery brought out with magic in *Hide and Seek*. He has carried this preoccupation with blood vessels into a series of X-ray visions of the human body which are peculiarly his own.

This is close to Surrealism, although Tchelitchew does not usually illustrate states of mind. The *Fish Bowl* was used as the central element in his monumental *Phenomena*, where it appears as a cell of acute self-consciousness in the midst of a welter of uncomfortable recollections.

Tchelitchew is an international figure, by temperament and experience; he came to America for the first time in 1934. The autumn countryside of Connecticut has had much to do with his present brilliant palette. He is a painter of infinite resource and taste, whose limitations lie in a certain fragility which deprives his work of power.

43. Fish Bowl, 1938

43

Eugene Berman: 1899-

There is a close parallel in the careers of Berman and Tchelitchew. Both are Russian, both left Russia after the Revolution, painted in Paris in the twenties and were exhibited together in the Neo-Romantic group that emerged in 1926. They had in common not only the mannered nostalgia of the group, with its low-keyed palette, but a limitless skill and facility with paint. Both have painted and designed for the theatre and ballet, and Berman, like Tchelitchew, moved to America in the thirties.

Berman was fascinated by architecture when he was a student in Russia, an interest which provided important elements in his painting, both as to subject, and as a source of organization and structure. His compositions possess architectural scale; they invite expansion, and their air of the theatre gives them their charm. The beholder is restricted to an aesthetic response, even when the painting is laden with grief.

The Neo-Romantics were under the spell of Picasso's Blue and Rose Periods, and of the early work of Chirico. Berman, like Chirico, was haunted by an ominous quietude, by architecture and by Italy. He visited Italy almost yearly in the twenties and thirties, and was enthralled by Venice and its painters, especially Tiepolo and Guardi. *Paludes* recalls these eighteenth-century masters even to the brushwork.

In the thirties Berman fell under the influence of Dali and Surrealism; he uses Surrealism, however, for its decorative rather than its shock effect. This catalogue of his resemblances to other painters is no impeachment of Berman's originality. His figures, motionless and entranced, placed theatrically in a limitless landscape, create a unique world of mournful reverie. If Berman has been influenced by many, he in turn has influenced others. Since he has been in America, his palette has grown more brilliant, in response to the color of the Southwest and of Mexico.

44. Paludes, 1937

Walter Stuempfig: 1914-

A romantic painter, Walter Stuempfig has a highly sensitive art not unrelated to that of such painters as Eugene Berman, and Berman's brother Leonid. There is the same deep space and skillful placing of languid figures. There are the same remembrances of the eighteenth-century Venetian painters, which come out strongly in Stuempfig's paintings of boats on quiet water.

If this were all, Stuempfig would be simply a decorative painter with taste. But his canvases are vivid with the sultry shore of Cape May and the Jersey coast; his scenes are bleached with the sun that drenches over sand, and over the gimcrack houses of another epoch; one sees the paint peeling, the nails rusting. All this, and the lives that go with the houses and boats, is described with understanding and without pathos.

Stuempfig is a Philadelphia painter. He studied at the Pennsylvania Academy of Fine Arts, and he has gone through an abstract period. One could hardly expect exuberance of a reporter in this moment of time, but Stuempfig is a philosopher rather than a moralist: he looks to the landscape environment, and draws strength and contentment from sun, air and sea even where man has done his worst to mar the scene. It is this warmth and glow in his landscape which lifts Stuempfig's painting into a major key. There is a slow tempo which may well be a sign of deep patience with existence, of mature understanding.

45. Two Houses, 1946

Karl Zerbe: 1903-

Karl Zerbe was born in Germany and brought up in France, where he went to school. Later he studied in Munich under a pupil of the Norwegian painter Munch; but France and Italy have had a strong influence on his work. He came to America in the mid-thirties.

With this background, Zerbe's painting shows the influence of twentieth-century German art and its exaggerated emotional content, along with a more formal feeling for the organization of space that an artist learns in France. The Germanic side of his painting contributes the strength; he appears to have seen France and Italy with the eyes of a Neo-Romantic. He has taken the Latin world as source-material for a romantic art, and has used architecture for its decorative effect.

Like the Neo-Romantics, Zerbe skirts the territory of Surrealism; he paints still-lifes, in which objects are brought together in that significant disorder which parallels the subconscious association of ideas. By this means he throws a bridge from the decorative to the more emotional side of his art, for the disparate objects, which provide entertainment for the eye, are also charged with symbolism.

A subdued palette and the use of black outline tend further to harmonize and knit together the complex elements in Zerbe's art. He can paint an excellent portrait. He has a great interest in techniques, and has employed the medium of encaustic, which in his hands is almost as tractable as oil. Zerbe has had a strong influence on the development of painting in Boston, where he has become an important teacher.

46. St. Louis Drawing Room, 1946

Louis Eilshemius: 1864-1941

The story of Louis Eilshemius is a tragedy in which poverty played no part; he was the son of a wealthy man. A desire for recognition, of normal proportions in the beginning, reached pathetic heights in the course of a frustrated life. The simplicity of his nature set a gulf of embarrassment between himself and others. In later life he thrust this embarrassment over onto his audience, when he became the self-styled Mahatma Eilshemius and loaded himself with the praises which had been denied him.

Eilshemius studied with Robert Minor, a painter trained in the Fontainebleau School under Diaz, and a sylvan lyricism was to persist in Eilshemius' work. He went to Paris in 1886, and when he returned to New York two years later the National Academy accepted two of his paintings, but it never did so again. Neither could he win admiration from his fellow painters—the long heartbreak had begun.

Eilshemius traveled widely: to Europe, North Africa, California, and to Samoa in 1901. Yet he was always drawn back to New York by his ambitions, and he courted fame with more than one art. He was both poet and musician, and he wrote short stories, novels and a fictionalized *Devil's Diary*, all privately printed. "Songs of Spring and Unrequited Love" is a revealing title, for his desires were unrequited on every level; he lived a bachelor whose shy fantasies were revealed in his verse, and his romantic attachments were for adolescent girls. He did succeed in reaching the public through communications to the newspapers, but these were treated as crank letters and grew more flamboyant over the years.

Eilshemius exhibited at the first Independents show in 1917. Marcel Duchamps was impressed, and through his interest the Société Anonyme showed Eilshemius twice, in 1920 and 1924. He had a one-man show in 1926, but the criticism was harsh and he was not shown again until 1932. There was another exhibition in Paris that same year. Eilshemius had now won through to success, but it came too late for him; it was like the rescue of King Lear.

Contentment was painted in a studio in Rome on one of Eilshemius' journeys. He has strewn the figures in a romantic dell: his landscapes are always felicitous. His poetic painting borders on the primitive in its direct simplicity and its innocence.

47. Contentment, 1903

126

John Kane: 1860-1934

All primitive painters are realists in that they wish to convince the beholder. When John Kane paints a landscape he undertakes to describe it in detail. In *Prosperity's Increase*, he is not concerned with laws of perspective; he is giving an account of what you will find in a certain landscape if you enter it by way of the bridge. The road in the foreground he helped pave; he took this road to the center of the bridge where he drew the middle section of the painting, in order to give us a nearer and more explicit account. Detail and description must fit: the hills must definitely be raised until they appear as hills, the houses must be large enough to be seen as houses; the flights of steps which climb the hillsides from street to street must be lifted out of experience into view. "When I see Pittsburgh," he said, "I see it with my recollections as well as the way it looks."

By the time Kane's account is complete it has an unconscious style. Kane has created a mesh of curving light lines out of the suspension bridge and the roads; he has held his painting together with its quiet tonalities; and he has communicated his absorption in the scene by the obvious pains he has taken with the work.

Kane was born in Scotland. By the age of ten he was a miner; at nineteen he came to America and worked at the blast furnaces at Connellsville and Bessemer, Pennsylvania. When this work grew too heavy for him he paved streets and later became a house-painter. He lived for the remainder of his life in Pittsburgh and, when he began to paint, the city became a constant subject.

Kane brought his paintings to the Carnegie Institute, where one was accepted for exhibition in 1927. From then on his reputation grew, and his work had appeared in many important exhibitions before his death.

48. Prosperity's Increase, 1933

Morris Hirschfield: 1872-1946

About the turn of the century, painters began to reach beyond the European tradition and became absorbed in primitive art. The art of the unschooled held a similar fascination, achieving its ends outside the framework of the cultural vision of the epoch. Finally, the role played by subconscious imagery in conveying the impact of works of art began to be understood.

Among our primitive painters, Kane is a realist of a tender mood; Pippin a poet; Hirschfield a painter of images heavily charged with sensuous symbolism. All his life he had labored to adorn women: he became head of a firm which made women's coats and suits, and later made a success of manufacturing "boudoir slippers." When he retired in his sixties he began shyly to paint.

The femininity of *Beach Girl*, of his first painting, *Girl in the Mirror*, and of *Nude at the Window*, is matched by another series which takes a masculine turn: *Angora Cat, Lion* (which is somehow a remarkable self-portrait), and *Tiger*. The subjects betray an intense, if obscure, emotional urgency. *Nude at the Window: Hot Night in July*—as it was originally titled—presents an intent young woman looking out through heavy red draperies. Her hands and feet are curiously infantile. The whole figure, afloat and tightly framed in a black void significantly the shape of a vase, appears about to be born. The only wearing apparel the artist offers her are the boudoir slippers which he had manufactured all his life. The scalloped and dotted red pattern edging the deep red curtains repeats the stylized forms of the breasts. The subconscious fantasy of the artist is working itself out, elaborating a meaningful design, quite as fully or pictorially as in any painting carried out in terms of the idiom of a cultural epoch. Hence the painting's vitality and concentration, its success as a creative work.

49. Nude at the Window, 1941

49

Horace Pippin: 1888-1946

"Pictures just come to my mind and I tell my heart to go ahead." There is little that can be added to this statement of Horace Pippin's to illuminate the work of an unschooled Negro painter.

Pippin wanted to paint remembered scenes; but he wanted still more to paint imagined scenes: he was a dramatist and poet with his brush. He wanted, of course, to be convincing, and his paintings carry an extraordinary conviction of reality—that this is how it was—precisely because the artist draws on his imagination. This is the world of fable. It is also in more exalted moments the world of religious painting. But all Pippin's work has a devout quality whether the subject is religious or not. The sense of rightness drawn from religious belief, and rightness in the composition and elaboration of a painting, are indistinguishable for Pippin. They are both spiritual satisfactions.

An account of his life simply reports on the humility of his earlier days and the pathos of his success. He grew up in Goshen, New York, where his mother worked as a servant. Pippin was a furniture packer and worked at a score of other odd jobs from the time of his mother's death in 1911 until he entered the Army in 1917. He kept a diary of his war service, and the war furnished him with subjects for a number of his paintings. He was sent to France, saw action, and was hit by a sniper's bullet which left him with a paralyzed right arm. Hence the leisure which led him quite casually toward painting. He did not begin to paint until he was forty-two.

Pippin lived in West Chester, Pennsylvania, where he was "discovered" in 1937. Four of his paintings were shown the following year at the Museum of Modern Art, and the Carlen Gallery in Philadelphia gave him an exhibition. From then on the New York galleries brought him forward, and it is remarkable that his naïve art survived his sudden success. His painting lost neither its dignity nor its innocence; but he was not so fortunate in his life, which became quite disorganized through his change of circumstances. He died suddenly in 1946.

50. Holy Mountain, II, 1944

List of Owners

Addison Gallery of American Art, Andover, Massachusetts
Art Institute of Chicago
City Art Museum of St. Louis
Cleveland Museum of Art
Corcoran Gallery of Art, Washington
Detroit Institute of Arts
Fogg Museum of Art, Harvard University
Metropolitan Museum of Art, New York
Museum of Fine Arts, Boston
Newark Museum, Newark, New Jersey
Philadelphia Museum of Art
Phillips Gallery, Washington
Whitney Museum of American Art, New York

Mr. and Mrs. Frederick B. Adams, Jr., New York
Benjamin Baldwin, Esq., New York
Edward A. Bragaline, Esq., New York
Mr. and Mrs. George Dangerfield, New York
Downtown Gallery, New York
Durand-Ruel, Inc., New York
Durlacher Brothers, New York
M. Martin Janis, Esq., Buffalo
C. H. Kleeman, Esq., New York
M. Knoedler and Company, New York
Yasuo Kuniyoshi, Esq., New York
Mr. and Mrs. Roy R. Neuberger, New York
William S. Paley, Esq., New York
A. P. Rosenberg and Company, New York
Robert and Joyce K. Rosenberg, White Plains, New York
Jacques Seligmann and Company, New York
James Thrall Soby, Esq., Farmington, Connecticut
Mr. and Mrs. Otto Spaeth, New York
Keith Warner, Esq., Fort Lauderdale, Florida
Karl Zerbe, Esq., Belmont, Massachusetts

Index of Painters

Printed by Clarke and Sherwell Limited Northampton England